Mushroom Wisdom

How Shaman Cultivate Spiritual Consciousness

Martin W. Ball, PhD

Ronin Publishing
Berkeley, California
www.roninpub.com

An excellent guide to the use of sacred mushrooms as tools in the quest for knowledge of the true self. A much needed contribution written in a clear unpretentious language that is obviously based on deep personal experience.

-- Luis Eduardo Luna, PhD

Fellow of the Linnean Society

author of
Vegetalismo,
Shamanism Among
the Mestizo Population
of the Peruvian Amazon

co-author of
Ayahuasca Visions
The Religious Iconography
of a Peruvian Shaman.

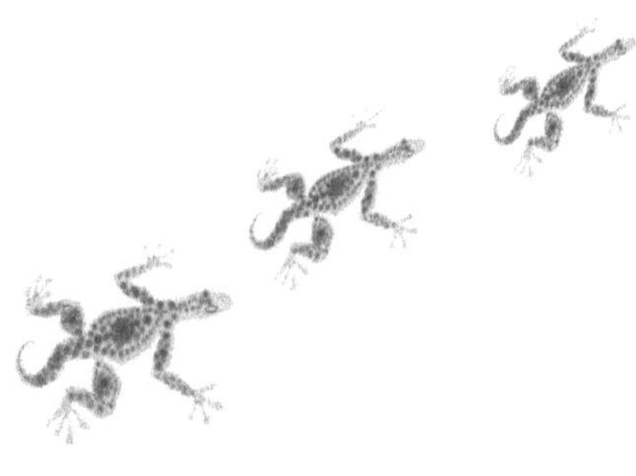

Mushroom Wisdom

How Shaman Cultivate Spiritual Consciousness

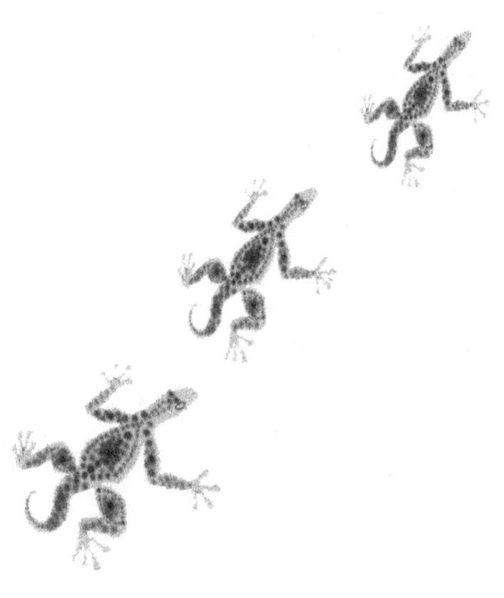

Mushroom Wisdom

ISBN: 978-1579-51036-7
E-ISBN: 978-1-57951-077-0

Published by
Ronin Publishing, Inc.
PO Box 3436
Oakland, CA 94609
www.roninpub.com

Production:
Editor: Beverly A. Potter (docpotter.com)
Cover Design: Beverly A. Potter
Cover Art: Martin W. Ball (martinball.net)
Book Design: Beverly A. Potter
Illustrations: Martin W. Ball

Fonts:
Papyrus: Esselle Letraset
BlownDeadline: Chank
MesoDeko: Deniart Systems
Venis: Chank

Library of Congress Card Number: 2006935886
Distributed by **Publishers Group West/Ingram**
Printed in the United States.

Table of Contents

Preface

Mushroom Wisdom is a summary of my best advice on using mushrooms and entheogens as agents of spiritual awareness, transformation and experience. It is about the being open, aware, and engaged in the transformative process that is the cultivation of spiritual consciousness. It is about facing darkness and overcoming the limitations of illusions, judgments, and the wounded emotions we carry in our hearts.

Eating entheogenic mushrooms is not for everyone. While many people enjoy these sacred sacraments as recreational entertainments and use them as a means to have fun and magical experiences, they can easily launch a person on a difficult, frightening, and often harrowing experience. Understanding their spiritual nature is not necessarily about having "good" trips and avoiding "bad" trips. It is about understanding how plant teachers can be used as the profound spiritual tools that they are and understanding how they work to impart their profound lessons.

> May those who
> seek find their way,
> embraced by the Spirit
> and bathed in the Light
> of consciousness and
> understanding.

This work is about how entheogenic experiences—good or bad, joyful or fearful, ecstatic or emotionally crushing—can be used as tools for spiritual growth. If one chooses to visit with such teachers and expose oneself to their lessons, shouldn't one approach the experience with knowledge, awareness, and an understanding of how navigate and make sense of the often overwhelming and radical phenomena that they open up for the spiritual seeker?

What one gets out of such experiences depends on the individual. Once a threshold amount is consumed, mushrooms radically alter perception, sense of being, and experience of self and world. Their value as spiritual tools, however, depends on the mindset, attitude, and disposition of the mushroom eater, and the framework and context in which they are consumed. What this means is that spiritual seekers take an active part in creating the sacredness of the experience. What one brings to the experience heavily influences what one gets out of it, though intentions and context never entirely determine the nature of the entheogen experience. What entheogens present is always new, profound, and beyond any attempt to control them, and that is part of their appeal and wonder. Eating psilocybin mushrooms opens one up to the profound and the spirit, intelligence, and power that exists within all things that manifest in the magical unfolding of the universe.

My purpose in this work is to help those who seek to better understand this process and the means through which these invaluable spiritual tools can be engaged and used to deepen spiritual awareness and experience to create more fully aware, accepting, and conscious spiritual beings.

-- Martin W. Ball

Mushroom space is a divine space, a space of paradoxes, spirit, mind, meaning, beauty, and wonder. It is intelligent and alive, organic, flowing, transformative, fluid, open, inviting, playful, serious, insightful, sacred. It is chaos and order, flux and change, ebb and flow, life and death, immanent and transcendent. It is beauty. It is home.

CHAPTER 1

Entheogens, Religion, and Spirituality

> They are the keys to the dimensions surrounding us that ordinarily cannot be seen. If they permit, you will be granted access to unimaginable dimensions of beauty, grace, and peacefulness. They bring me closer to God, Jesus, Buddha, Gaian consciousness, my origins, and to a deeper understanding of my purpose in the universe. The experience, by all measures, is profoundly spiritual.
>
> -- Paul Stamets

AROUND THE GLOBE and throughout history, plant teachers have had profound and lasting effects on cultures, traditions, religions, and individual experiences of spirituality and the sacred. Often strange and wondrous, plant teachers, or entheogens, plants that evoke "God within," are capable of catapulting human consciousness out of the mundane and into the spiritually profound, bringing direct connection to the sacred and the divine. This basic fact has been used by countless cultures to deepen individual experiences of the sacred, from initiation into religious mysteries to shamanic healing, divination, and spiritual journeying.

While the experiences generated by entheogens are not necessarily spiritual or religiously meaningful in and of themselves, if attended to with the proper mind set with the proper intention and consumed in a context of sacredness and spirituality, they can be powerful catalysts for spiritual growth and development. While not everyone who consumes entheogens becomes spiritually awakened or transformed, many are, and those with knowledge of the workings of these sacred plants, the shamans, mystics, and visionaries, have developed methods and techniques that serve to help guide others on their spiritual, religious, or healing paths.

Simply consuming a sacred plant does not make one a mystic.

Methods abound throughout history and across cultures for contacting the sacred or generating deep spiritual experiences, some of which are more effective than others. Techniques such as fasting, prolonged meditation, seclusion, physical stress, exercises and breathing methods, for example, have been used for millennia to generate spiritual experiences. Entheogens, while not necessarily inherently generative of spiritual experience, are often far more reliable and consistent than these other methods, however, in generating radical and profound experiences. Shamans have known for thousands of years that certain plants, when prepared and consumed in the proper set and setting with the necessary attention to ritual, structure, and intention, can be fairly consistently relied upon to produce profound and life-altering spiritual experiences in all manner of people from laypersons to ritual experts. It is quite possible that these

other techniques of meditation, breathing, isolation, fasting, and so forth are later attempts to recreate the entheogen experience through other means.

Simply consuming a sacred plant such as peyote, mushrooms, ayahuasca (which is technically not an individual plant but a synthesis of various species), datura, iboga, s*alvia divinorum*, or any other such plant, does not automatically make one a mystic, a shaman, or bring one to the far side of enlightenment. Sacred plants do not engender spiritual awakening out of necessity. While there are always examples of people who consume such plants and are spontaneously catapulted into profound states of spiritual awareness, there are plenty of counter examples of people who become confused, tormented, and lost, or even more mundanely, simply have "fun." What this indicates it that the cultivation of spiritual awareness with entheogens is something that generally requires work. This work includes inculcating the proper mind set and intention, creating the proper space for the experience, and the use of various tools and methodologies to both navigate and make sense of the often confusing and unexpected realms that entheogens make accessible to the spiritual seeker, mystic, and shamanic practitioner.

Cultivating spiritual awareness requires work.

In sum, entheogens are profound spiritual tools, but like any tool, one must know how to use them if one hopes to achieve specific results. In traditional cultures, it is the shamans, mystics, seers, ritual priests and priestesses, who possess the necessary knowledge to guide others through the labyrinthine experience of

entheogens. These experts know how to find their own way through strange and wondrous realities and know how to guide others through as well, bringing them to the state of awareness, health, happiness, or insight that they seek. The practice of such individuals is an art of the highest degree and makes use of intentions, thoughts, sounds, symbols, ritual, and countless other factors to generate the sought after experiences and realizations.

Discovering Entheogen-Based Wisdom

MANY IN THE WEST are only exposed to such gifted individuals in very limited contexts, if at all. Access to mind expanding plants and chemicals abound, but clear understandings of how these tools are used for spirituality is rare. Westerners who have an interest in traditional uses of entheogens travel the globe to meet with Amazonian shamans for ayahuasca sessions, or make a pilgrimage high into the mountains of Mexico to learn of *salvia divinorum* from the Mazatec, or peyote from the Huichol. Such a journey is a luxury, however, and it is not very practical to tell someone who wants to learn the uses of sacred plants to pack up and go to the Amazon.

Shamanic tourism is great business and helps support local, indigenous populations, but must one travel the world for spiritual insight and experience, especially when the shamans generally all insist that the knowledge is right there for anyone to access, at least in some form, if not the specific cultural form that it takes in different cultures and communities? If the knowledge is really "out there," shouldn't anyone be able to tap into it, at any time, at any place?

This work here is meant as an investigation into the above question. The general hypothesis here is that spiritual experience is available to anyone who seeks it, and knowledge of how to use sacred plants can be learned and taught, at least at a general level, without having to travel the world, seeking out the last lonely places where the secret mysteries reside. Spiritual experience is right here, right now. It isn't something that has to be far away, secret, or exotic. It's the closest possible thing, really, because spiritual reality is the real reality. The world of Spirit is what truly is.

I felt awaken and inspired.

Finding Authenticity

FOR MANY in the postmodern west, genuine spirituality is often something difficult to achieve with a sense of authenticity. There are many seekers and there are many paths, some more successful than others. Many turn to use of entheogens to enhance their sense of spiritual awareness and expand their consciousness. As with other paths, there are different levels of success to such practices.

I count myself as one who had difficulty finding an authentic path to spiritual awareness. My spiritual life underwent a radical revolution one day after I had eaten 3.2 grams of dried psilocybin mushrooms. While I had experimented with mushrooms prior to this, this time was different. I underwent what I can best describe as a shamanic initiation, guided by the mushrooms themselves. I emerged from the experience with a profoundly transformed sense of spirituality and I felt awakened and inspired in way I couldn't have described before. Spiritual experience went from something abstract and intellectually stimulating to something that was a part of who I was. This book is a meditation on how I have come to think of mushrooms, religion, and spirituality in the decade since that initiation experience. It is not meant to advocate that anyone use mushrooms or do anything to break any laws. Rather, this is a personal reflection on how the experiences engendered by psilocybin mushrooms can contribute to spiritual growth and development.

Experiential Knowledge

THE PRACTICAL SPIRITUALITY PRESENTED HERE is not dependent on any particular theory or system. In fact, in some sense there is no theory here at all. Spiritual experience simply is. It is a fact that must be taken at face value. All speech about spiritual experience is a reconstruction after the fact. The more advanced our knowledge or our conceptual system, the more subtly we may be able to describe our experience to others or to ourselves, but the experience itself is not dependent on the theory or the language used to articulate it. Direct spiritual experience immediately shows us the limits of our own concepts and knowledge. What is important is the experience itself.

> Spiritual experience simply is.

Knowledge based on direct and immediate experience is radically different from intellectual knowledge, and anyone who has had such an experience knows this to be true. Thus the discussion in this book is focused on the nature of these experiences, how spiritual seekers are able to navigate them, and what they mean and how they can be used in individuals' development as spiritual beings.

Spirituality without Religion

THIS IS NOT A WORK about any particular religion in any way. While there are religions and cultures that have used mushrooms as part of their practice, this is not about any of them. Mushrooms are a spiritual tool that is available to anyone of any religion, or even, as in my case, no religion at all. Cultures that use or have used mushrooms tend to use them shamanistically, which, while certainly connected to the superstructures of cultural belief systems, is primarily a system of practice based on direct experience and heightened perception. However, there is plenty written out there in anthropological literature about cultures that use mushrooms and their belief systems and styles of practice. This book is not about any particular tradition or culture's approach to using mushrooms, though there will no doubt be parallels.

You need not be religious to be spiritual.

It should also be made clear at the outset that the concepts of "religion" and "spirituality" are considered to be rather distinct in this work. For the purposes of this work, "religion" is more closely associated with communally held beliefs, practices, and social structures. "Spirituality" is based on direct experience, is open to multiple interpretations, and is not dependent on any particular system of belief, dogma, or religious creed. In short, one need not be religious to be spiritual, and conversely, being religious is not necessarily identical to being spiritual or having genuine spiritual experience.

Why this Book?

AS GENUINE SPIRITUAL KNOWLEDGE IS, in some sense, out there," and is not confined to any one tradition, culture, or religion, nothing written here is in any way new, original, or unique. The kinds of spiritual techniques, practices, and experiences that are found here have been recounted in countless forms of literature from anthropology, history of religions, spirituality, self-help guides, weekend workshops, shamanistic and metaphysical writings, the Enneagram, and others. With that said, however, there is no concise work elucidating how these ideas immediately relate to the use of mushrooms as a system of practice and spiritual methodology. There is plenty of "psychedelic" literature available for the interested reader, but there is not an in-depth investigation specifically related to mushroom consciousness and spiritual practice and experience, at least, not that I know of.

Mushrooms are profound spiritual tools, but many who consume mushrooms do not appreciate their full potential in this capacity. Merely consuming psychedelic mushrooms does not make a person a mystic or a shaman, nor even necessarily more spiritual. Mushrooms can provide very entertaining and profound experiences. There are beautiful colors, the geometric forms are mesmerizing, and the experience can be aesthetically rapturous. But these are not the hallmarks of using mushrooms as a tool. A tool implies purpose, function, and use. That is what this work will emphasize. Anyone can eat mushrooms and experience the profound mind-manifesting powers of the sacred plant, but actually using them with intent and purpose for spiritual development and awareness requires certain techniques.

We may ask, if the knowledge being shared here is available elsewhere and in other forms, why this study? Aside from the fact that no such work currently exists, there are other reasons. Spiritual practice is difficult and challenging. Often growth and development can be slow, if at all. People can spend years sitting in meditation and get nothing but sleepy. People can go to church their whole lives and not have anything more than the dogma of their tradition to base their spirituality on. Mushrooms, on the other hand, are imme-

Entheogens open up the possibility of a deep spiritual experience.

diate, radical, and direct. In some sense, mushrooms, and other entheogens, when used correctly, are great spiritual equalizers in that they make profound states of spiritual consciousness available to nearly anyone. Given this, knowledge of such practices can be deemed to be significant to humanity in general, and spiritual seekers in particular, especially given widespread misunderstandings of "hallucinogens" and their relationship to spirituality and religion.

The spiritual equalization made available to users of entheogens does not necessarily imply that mushroom-derived spirituality is easy or simple, for it isn't, but does imply that entheogens open up the possibility of deep spiritual experience for those who might not otherwise be open to spirituality. It is also not meant as an encouragement of anyone to consume mushrooms. However, simply as a testament to the variety of spiritual experience, a study like this should be available, if for no other reason. An ordinary mushroom that reveals so much is worthy of investigation simply because it exists, let alone for what it engenders.

A study such as this is also important as mushrooms, and other similar mind-expanding plant teachers, are largely criminalized and outlawed in our culture. This is a profound disservice to our culture and is a radical infringement on our spiritual freedom. Honest assessment of these powerful plant teachers cannot take place in an atmosphere of misinformation, social dogma, and

> There is no scret, no mysterious truth or hidden enigma to be revealed.

outright demonization of sacred plants. Our consciousness and spiritual natures are the most intimate aspects of our being, and the presumption that anyone can deny you the access to the depths of your own mind and spirit is what is indeed criminal. Exploration of consciousness and spirituality, when undertaken in responsible and affirming contexts, is a human right of the highest degree and is inalienable.

No Secrets

THERE IS NO SECRET, no mysterious truth, no hidden enigma to be revealed. Mushrooms allow spiritual seekers to do one basic thing: They help the seeker to understand his or her true nature. While structured religions are about a great many things, at their spiritual core, all religions point back to this same basic truth in that they teach us who we are, our relationship to the sacred, to the world, and the other beings we find within it. At the deepest level, there is only one thing. Our views of ourselves as distinct and separate beings are ultimately illusions and constructs of the mind. At heart, we are all one; everything is one.

The universe itself is a living, conscious being, that uses space and time to manifest itself in creative expressions of life and development. In the end, we, as conscious and thinking beings, are the universe reflecting back on itself. Our spiritual core is one and all of existence is just different facets and manifestations of this one, undivided, all encompassing whole. Some call this "God." I call it the universe. Others give it different names. Names, terms, or concepts don't matter. It is all about experience. For those who have had such an experience, the truth of the proposition is undeniable.

It may be doubted later, but when one returns to the experience, one knows it to be true again. The deeper one goes, the more one sees that this truth is evident everywhere. In other words, there is nothing unique about the profound revelations of the mushroom experience, because it never stops. The mushrooms just make clear and evident what we forget to remember in our ordinary consciousness. The mushrooms remind us of the real and show us who and what we really are. The experience of the mushrooms and the other plant teachers is the experience of reality and our true nature as spiritual beings.

The Shaman's Path to Spirit

SHAMANIC PRACTICE, unlike many forms of religiosity, is primarily based on direct spiritual experience. Sound, movement, symbols, and methods of engaging the senses are all used by shamans to generate deeply spiritual experiences for a variety of purposes, from personal enlightenment to healing. Shamans were, and are, the first masters of the entheogen experience, and in many respects, the plant teachers cre[illegible] shamans through their own initiations. Thus many of the specific technique[illegible]d approaches discussed in this work are similar to, or related to, practices mastered by shamans around the globe and across history.

This is not a work about necessarily becoming a shaman, however, and thus we should distinguish between using shamanic techniques and actually holding the title of a "shaman." A shaman is someone who generally works within a traditional context, using cultural symbols, stories, and ritual practices, to achieve set aims for his or her community, such as healing, influencing events, and mediating between communities of humans and non-human entities, including spirits, animals, plants, and geographical forms such as rivers and mountains.

One need not be a "shaman" to use shamanic techniques. Given that shamanism most likely developed out of archaic experiences with plant teachers, it is only natural that shamanic methodologies and understandings are fruitful and productive when looking to use entheogens for the cultivation of spiritual consciousness and spiritual experiences. Anyone of any religion or system of belief can use shamanic methodologies for the purpose of deepening his or her spiritual experience and understanding as they are ultimately practical. They are meant to be applied directly to spiritual practice and experience. In the end, all such techniques and methodologies must be made one's own, for shamanic practice is deeply personal and involves an exploration and development of one's creativity at a spiritual level. In that sense, the exploration of shamanic spirituality can be intensely creative and personally rewarding, for as one comes to a deeper and more authentic sense of self and being, so too does one's sense of creativity and expression become more authentic and profound, which in turn leads to more fulfilling and profound relationships to one's self, others, the earth, and all the inhabitants of our spiritually resonate universe.

Chapter 1, Main Points

* Using mushrooms as a spiritual tool implies purpose, intent, and work.

* Using mushrooms as a spiritual tool is distinct from using mushrooms for "fun."

* Spiritual experience is distinct from religion.

* Spiritual experience is direct and immediate.

* All descriptions of spiritual experiences are reconstructions after the fact.

* Language, beliefs, theories, religions, are all constructs of the human mind and are not necessarily "reality."

* Direct experience is far more important than theories or dogma.

* There are specific techniques than can be shared to use mushrooms spiritually.

* Using mushrooms as a spiritual tool is fundamentally about facing one's self, overcoming illusions, and regaining a deeper, spiritual sense of self and connection to the sacred.

CHAPTER 2

The Mushroom Experience

MUSHROOMS TEND TO MANIFEST in similar ways regardless of amount or potency. There are similar qualities of the experience that seem to be fairly consistent with both weak and strong experiences, and these are the qualities that are the focus here.

The potency of psilocybin mushrooms varies greatly from one mushroom to the next. Three grams of one batch of mushrooms might be mild and hardly noticeable in their effect, whereas one gram of a really strong mushroom might send one on a five-hour journey of intense introspection and mystical wonder. Other than knowing the relative potencies of different varieties

> Our consciousness changed many times during that night. It seemed we all changed together, which I attribute to the control Santa Maria exerted over us. The states of consciousness seemed to vary with the rhythm of her chants.
>
> -- Frederick Swain
>
> Session with Maria Sabina
> Mazatec Mushroom Sham

of psilocybin mushrooms, there is no general way to assess whether any given mushroom will be highly potent or weak. In the end, direct experience is the only real measure.

A small amount of mushrooms can be as effective for spiritual work as a large amount.

If one is seeking to learn from mushrooms, it is actually easier to understand what is happening with somewhat larger or stronger doses. It is not that the experience is necessarily qualitatively different with higher does—only that it is more obvious and less subtle and therefore allows one to go deeper into the experience with a more immediate and intuitive understanding of what is happening and why. For an inexperienced mushroom eater, however, large doses can be difficult to navigate and potentially overwhelming, producing profoundly confusing states of consciousness, incoherence, and accompanying odd behavior. For that reason, experienced mushroom eaters recommend that those who wish to pursue mushroom experiences should start with a small amount and work up to a level that is comfortable.

Many approach mushrooms with the goal of consuming enough to cross the visual threshold where the aesthetic rapture of the mushrooms takes hold. Most people want "visuals" as part of their trip. *Mushroom Wisdom* has a different emphasis. What is important is how the mushroom eater approaches and works with the experience. Even a very small amount of mushrooms can be as effective for spiritual work as a large amount, when mushroom eaters know what they are doing. Ideally, if one were skilled enough with these techniques and practices, mushrooms would not be needed at all. Indeed, this would be the eventual goal—to have mushrooms open one up to spiritual perception and insight at a deeply personal level, and then integrate such perception and action into normal

life. While mushroom states of consciousness are highly refined and often transcendent and profound, the ultimate goal is to bring these insights into everyday life. That is the goal of any form of spiritually transformative work.

That Earthy Flavor

MUSHROOMS CAN BE EATEN, made into tea, chopped up, or strained, however the mushroom eater might like according to preference and taste. There are reports of people smoking mushrooms, but the effectiveness of such a practice is in dispute.

Most people find the taste of mushrooms unpleasant. They have a very earthy taste, like dirt and mulch mixed together with a damp forest floor. As with many things, enjoying the flavor of mushrooms is an acquired taste and many never get past the unpleasant flavors. To mask the flavor, making tea with mint, lemon, or honey are common techniques. Some brew the mushrooms in the tea for an hour or so and then strain the mushrooms and drink just the remaining tea.

I favor actually consuming the mushrooms themselves. There seems to be a difference between taking the mushroom into one's body versus taking an extract or tea. There is also the ritual sense of taking communion, or sharing in a sacrament when the mushroom body is ingested and this tends to promote feelings of symbiotic relationship between the eater and the mushroom.

Mushrooms taste like dirt and mulch mixed together with a damp forest floor.

When mushrooms are eaten, there is often the urge to get

them out of one's mouth and into one's stomach as soon as possible, given their taste. While tempting, the best advice is to take the time to chew them thoroughly. Mushrooms are not easy to digest and the more work done in the mouth, the better, as it is easier on the digestive track.

That Gut Feeling

MUSHROOM EATERS FEEL THE MUSHROOMS at work in the digestive track in varying degrees of intensity for the duration of the experience, and possibly beyond. They tend to produce gas, from both ends, and this can last for a while, especially towards the end of the experience. While many find the gustatory component uncomfortable, it is an important aspect of the experience and like all things with mushroom experiences, should be embraced. Fighting against something while under the influence of mushrooms is a losing effort. It is those who fight against the discomfort who tend to throw up. Those who must purge usually feel better after they've vomited and can then move more freely into the experience.

Mushroom eaters are wise to pay careful attention to what happens in their gut while in the experience. The gut is an important matrix of our emotions and all aspects of the mushroom experience have an emotional component. To learn what one's physical sensations mean and the emotional baggage they bring, the mushroom eater must pay attention and explore the experience.

There is a relationship between the "gut feeling" of mushrooms, and the "gut feeling" of intuition. Mushrooms open up the explorer to profoundly radical levels of intuition and empathic understanding that some describe as telepathy or psychic communication. These intuitions and revelatory insights often come accompanied by sensations of mushrooms working their way through the digestive tract. It is an interesting, though not at all surprising, correlation. Having a "gut feeling" about a person, place, situation, question, or quandary, takes on all new meaning when mushrooms are involved. The best advice for mushroom eaters is to pay careful attention to this correlation and use good judgment about what messages are being received from the psychic visitor moving through their body.

The Uncanny

STRONG MUSHROOMS START TO COME ON within a couple minutes and experienced users can usually identify a shift in consciousness very early on—sometimes even before eating the mushrooms. Weak mushrooms may take forty-five minutes or more to begin to really manifest, and even then only subtly. The first sensation is often one of "something is different," or "something is happening to me," but one might not yet be able to fully appreciate or understand what it is—only that something has changed and an inevitable, but difficult to define, process has begun.

Many find this uncanny state to be a difficult phase of the mushroom experience. Limbs may become heavy and mushroom eaters might have trouble moving and coordinating their bodies. Speech is difficult and sometime impossible. Language, in fact, can become very strange indeed. One begins to feel how putting thoughts and experiences into words affects reality. Words become heavy and filled with meaning, powerfully potent and potentially dangerous. One might realize that choice of words commits one to a particular view of reality and all

Mushrooms open up the explorer to profoundly radical levels of intuition and empathic understanding.

the additional commitments that come with such a view. For some, because of this potency of language, silence is taken up as the mode of choice. For others, they feel themselves mouthpieces for the mushrooms and get caught up in the liquid flow of mushroom language. Either way, most mushroom eaters agree that language, speech, and words are potent and profound and the conscious mushroom eater is reminded of the importance of using speech and language responsibly and with integrity and care.

The palms of the hands might become quite clammy and it is difficult to regulate body temperature as the mushrooms begin to manifest themselves. Hot and cold take on whole new meanings and the slightest breeze can alter the experience in surprising ways. For those who have a difficult time adjusting, or who are made uncomfortable by clammy hands, water is a great cure. Putting the hands in water, or even taking a shower, can be profoundly vitalizing. Eventually, the awkwardness passes, however, and a new equilibrium is established. Mushroom eaters become comfortable in their new body and new mind. This transition should not be fought or resisted as it only makes it more difficult.

Water on skin can be profoundly vitalizing.

Loss of Control

A COMMON PERCEPTION is that the mushroom eater is losing control. In many respects, this is true. "Me," that conventional sense of self and world is being overcome by something else, something both totally other and completely intimate. The "me" that is losing control is the self-created sense of self and the self-projected sense of reality. The mushroom eater's mind is opening.

Once the mushrooms take hold, the seeker experiences him or her self in an entirely new way, with a new mind and new body, though paradoxically, this is often accompanied by the feeling that "this is how it always is." This total perception of "otherness" and intimate sense of "homecoming" cannot be adequately described or articulated. One simply has to experience it to understand it. It's like remembering something that has been forgotten, but always known, even if only subliminally.

The "me" that is losing control is one's self-created sense of self and one's self-projected sense of reality.

A bad trip can be triggered by the urge to fight against losing control. There are few things that can produce as much anxiety as feeling one's carefully constructed sense of self being deconstructed by mushrooms. It feels like something is taking over and the self has been launched on a journey that cannot be stopped. This is a fundamental truth that should be accepted from the beginning.

Regaining Control

AS THE MUSHROOM EXPERIENCE PROGRESSES, the seeker regains control. In fact, quite paradoxically (as are so many things with mushrooms), when used correctly, mushroom eaters find that they have more direct control than during ordinary states of consciousness. Like a waking into lucid dreams where dreamers find that they can change and alter every aspect of the dreaming experience at will, so too mushroom eaters find the mushroom experience. There is nothing that cannot be changed or altered by a conscious intent of will in the mushroom experience. The difficulty is that this process is first losing control of safe reality constructions of the self and regaining a deeper sense of control from a deeper and subtler sense of self and identity. This may be what death is like. Ego-identity dissolves away to reveal the being of light hidden within and covered by illusions of a separate and isolated self. Everyone fears death. It is only natural that we fear a process of dissolution. This is not to say that eating mushrooms is as intense and profound as dying (how could anyone know?), but it may be similar. Approaching it with this understanding can be helpful. The mushroom eater should try not to be fearful and should accept what comes. Once the new body-mind of mushrooms has been assumed, a new and profound level of control can be established, but it takes some time.

Riding the Mushroom Waves

SOMETHING ALL EXPERIENCED MUSHROOM EATERS KNOW, but that the inexperienced often find surprising, is that mushroom experience comes in waves. As they start to come on, the waves are subtle and difficult to perceive or contemplate. This is the "something is happening but I don't know what" stage, which quickly progresses to "everything's moving!" and "look at the colors!", if the mushrooms are strong enough. The waves most often generate from the abdomen, or more precisely, where the mushrooms are in the body. Mushroom waves are multifaceted. They affect all aspects of being. There is a visual component, a cognitive component, a physical component, an emotional component, and a spiritual component. Each wave reaches its natural peak and then fades away, only to be replaced by another wave, though experienced mushroom users know how to shape waves so that they can be diminished or prolonged.

At some point the mushroom eater reaches the peak experience, often within the first hour or two. This is when the mushrooms are the strongest. The waves build up in intensity and frequency, much like a gathering storm. They then break over one's consciousness and being. The seeker is now fully in the mushroom experience. The peak can be very disorienting. Mind and emotions are not where they are normally expected to be. Bodily and spatial limits are overcome. The mushroom eater *is* the experience of the mushrooms, not a brain inside a body. The mushroom eater is the patterns, the colors, the thoughts, the emotions, the dreams that sweep over one. If it is a particularly intense mushroom experience, they may lose all sense of their immediate physical body. Some describe it as an "out of body" experience. For others it might be the experience of taking up all the space inside a room, forest grove, or mountain or sky. In other words, it can be both dislocating and expansive.

After the peak, the waves last longer and are gentler. Depending on the strength and amount of mushrooms consumed, this gradual decline of the experience can take one to several hours. Weaker mushrooms last for maybe two or three hours while more potent mushrooms might be five to six hours, or even more, depending on the amount consumed. The gentler declining waves are much easier to work with than the earlier waves leading up to the peak. In fact, at this point, it is possible to exert a fair amount of control over the waves. One can summon them up, or push them back, if needed. Concentrating makes the waves more intense. If attention is caught by something else, they recede into the background. They can also be amplified by resonating with the waves, such as through chanting, drumming, rattling, or playing droning instruments such as a di-

The waves build up in intensity and frequency, much like a gathering storm.

djeridu. Most mushroom eaters having a good experience try to prolong the waves to get as much out of them as possible, not wanting the magical experience to end.

Eventually the waves become so subtle that they simply wash away and mushroom eaters find themselves back in a normal state of consciousness. They re-establish habitual cognitive and emotional boundaries as they become "myself" once more. If the mushroom eater has done it right, however, and used the mushrooms as a tool, and not just as an entertaining light and psychic show, he or she will have a completely different understanding of who this person called "me" actually is, and his or her view of the world and all things in it could be profoundly altered as well.

Visuals, Emotions, and Thoughts

NO DISCUSSION OF ANY ENTHEOGEN EXPERIENCE would be complete without addressing the issue of their visual nature. Leaving aside the issue of "hallucinations" for the moment, the visual aspect of entheogens is a primary aspect of the experience. Different entheogens produce different kinds of visual experiences as do different varieties of related entheogens. Ayahuasca is famous for producing visions of jaguars and serpents. DMT launches the explorer into completely other worlds. Datura is known for producing radical visions of the spirit world. And different varieties of mushrooms produce different effects depending on species, strength, and dosage.

At very low doses, the visual effects of mushrooms are very subtle. Colors become more vivid and light takes on a luminous, ethereal quality. Slight distortions in the visual field present themselves, but only subtly.

As the dosage and strength of the mushrooms increase, so do the visual effects. At slightly higher doses, patterns begin to appear on the surface of objects. When these effects first start to come on, I usually find myself thinking that the "mystic lizards" are here, given that the patterns the visuals create are very similar to M. C. Escher artwork of entwined lizards or other repeating patterns. Objects also begin to visually flow and melt with movement being the most defining characteristic of these visuals. All the world becomes movement, change, and flow. Light becomes extremely beautiful at this point and can be endlessly engrossing.

As the dosage and strength of the mushrooms increase, so do the visual effects.

At still higher doses and potency the visuals become even stronger. Patterns of flow, movement, and change are no longer confined to the surface of objects, but can fill all of the visual space of a person's perception. Empty rooms become filled with intricate lattices of undulating geometric patterns. The sky appears filled with energy currents and the depths of the heavens take on the appearance of magnificent architecture. Kaleidoscopic and mandala-like images abound.

At these doses, it is common to perceive oneself as embodied in these different patterns as the normal sense of one's physical body is transcended. Spiritual explorers may feel themselves as geometric shapes filling a room or extending on out into space. Scenes may also begin to unfold in these visions, complete with characters, architecture, and other places and other times. The geometric forms can also coalesce into definite figures or personas that may interact with the visionary or may present a form of communication.

At the highest doses, the physical world melts away and one becomes completely immersed in the visionary world of the mushrooms. Profound states of consciousness are reached therein and revelations and awakenings are common. Deep levels of synaesthesia are also reached where sounds, colors, smells, movements, and all the senses cross over into each other, opening the visionary up to radically altered ways of experiencing and appreciating the senses and their methods of processing information.

At the highest doses the physical world melts away. One is completely immersed in the visionary world of the mushrooms.

The visual aspects of mushrooms are beautiful and can be infinitely engrossing. They fill the world with a profound sense of wonder and awe, revealing the magic and mystery that embraces all things. Nature takes on a deep living quality and all things are perceived as expressive, alive, and intelligent. It is a true opening to the mystical powers of the mind and human awareness.

However, it is important to stress that the visual aspects of the mushrooms are intimately tied to all other aspects of the experience. Mushrooms are a complete somatic, emotional, and psychic experience. In this sense, the visuals are always tied to changes in cognition, body experience, and emotional experience. Really, there is no neutral aspect of the experience, as it is all tied together into a unified totality. This leads to a profound sense of meaning and significance to all that the visionary encounters on the journey. At times, this sense of meaning can feel overwhelming. Every aspect of the experience carries significance and communicates information to the visionary, filling the spirit with a sense of revelation and pure profundity.

Mushroom Space

MUSHROOM SPACE IS A DIVINE SPACE, a space of paradoxes, spirit, mind, meaning, beauty, and wonder. It is totally other and unknown, yet immediately familiar and intimate. It is an ephemeral dream, but also completely real and imbued with a sense of truth and fundamental reality.

It is intelligent and alive, organic, flowing, transformative, fluid, open, inviting, playful, serious, insightful, sacred. It is a space of knowledge and fascination, otherworldly awe and immediacy, overflowing with intuition, lessons to be learned, things forgotten, things unknown. It is a space of light and sound, wind and water, voices and images, flowing and changing, an eternal dance of becoming.

Mushroom space is a divine space, a space of paradoxes, spirit, mind, meaning, beauty, and wonder.

It is the matrix of perception, the matrix of being, the constant pulse of creation and life, consciousness, and spirit. It is the space of the ultimate Mind, the interconnectivity of all things, the spirit of life, of higher consciousness, of alien intelligence, of hyperdimensional star seeds of awareness. It is the vastness of the omniverse, a great ocean of vibration, the great music of existence. It carries within it information of all things in all times in all places, for it is the web of existence.

It is communication. It is a space of knowledge and sharing. It is the space that pulls away the masks of all limitations to reveal the world as a living presence, intelligent, purposeful, knowing, and compassionate.

Within this space, all things come to be, following their paths, returning to the source of Spirit, rising and falling together in great harmony, all part of the same whole, the same organic being, the same unity, the same totality. It is chaos and order, flux and change, ebb and flow, life and death, immanent and transcendent. It is beauty.

Chapter 2, Main Points:

* Mushrooms can be consumed as tea or eaten.

* Spiritual seekers have to find the amount and potency that is right for them.

* The onset of mushrooms can be disorienting and anxiety producing.

* Mushrooms come on in waves. They build in intensity and frequency until the "peak" experience, at which point they begin their gradual decline.

* Mushroom waves often appear to start in the abdomen and sweep through one's being.

* Mushroom waves can be influenced and explored.

* Exploring and directing mushroom waves is a form of spiritual practice when done with intention and spiritual awareness.

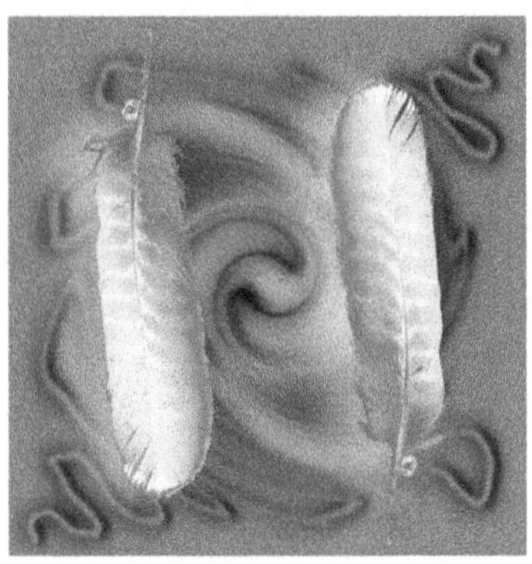

CHAPTER 3

Mushrooms as Psychedelic Experience

MUSHROOMS and other mind-altering substances have many labels in Western culture. Mushrooms are considered "hallucinogens" in the mainstream, implying that what is experienced under their influence is fundamentally not real. What is seen and experienced is supposedly a "hallucination"—things that are not there, impressions that do not have any reality content and are imaginary. The corollary to this bias is that all revelations, insights, or truths discovered while under the influence of mushrooms are illusory and basically false. At best, mushrooms are seen as hedonistic absorption, living in a fantasyland made of wishes and dreams. Perhaps they are entertaining, but the experience carries

> . . . ordinary perception was enriched and enlivened beyond comparison. It was clearly false that these drugs are "hallucinogenic" in the sense of hallucinating something that isn't there.
> -- Ralph Metzner

no value or deeper meaning beyond revealing the subjective workings of an individual's mind and imagination.

> I was immediately master of myself and my surroundings. I realized that everything is a state of mind. I am free and master of myself. I am whatever I believe myself to be, if my belief is strong enough. My mind was released from its struggle and I felt the strength of a giant, like a god. Yes, this was it, the real moment of truth.
> -- Frederick Swain

A basic premise of *Mushroom Wisdom* is that the "hallucinogenic" view is incorrect and fundamentally flawed. True, one can experience fantastic imagery and strange sense impressions, but labeling mushrooms as a hallucinogen is not the most useful when considering the spiritual properties of the experience. The *Mushroom Wisdom* perspective is that what is experienced while under the influence of mushrooms is fundamentally *more real* than the experience of ordinary consciousness.

Constructs of the Mind

HOW CAN IT BE that what is experienced under the influence of mushrooms is more real than ordinary consciousness? At the surface, this view seems absurd, given the powerful nature of mushrooms and the effects they produce on consciousness and perception. Fantastical imagery flows through wildly distorted thought processes, leading individuals to unlikely conclusions and ephemeral insights. How can this reveal the true nature of the mind and perception, when it is so obviously a distortion?

"Ordinary consciousness" is largely a product of our minds, our concepts, and our habits. What we normally perceive and contemplate about ourselves, the world about us, and others in it is a product of the constructs, beliefs, and judgments of our own minds. The world as we see it, including ourselves, is a representation that we create based on our sensory input, our beliefs, our values, our emotions, our concepts, our habitual ways of organizing experience. In a sense, we never actually *see* anything. We see an image in our minds that is constructed by our intellect to represent the world. It is a product. It is never the real thing in the world.

There is a chemical aspect of consciousness. Our faculty of mind is radically altered by body chemistry, and when entheogens are consumed, the chemical substrate of consciousness is directly affected. Ordinary consciousness can be viewed as more likely to produce accurate sense impressions as it functions within normal chemical parameters.

A natural counter-point to the chemical argument is that many entheogens merely produce chemicals that occur naturally in the brain. Tryptamines—the active components of mushrooms—are composed of chemicals manufactured naturally in the human brain, and are associated with various "natural" states of consciousness such as deep meditation, dreaming, out-of-body, and near death experiences. When taking this fact into consideration, it looks more like the active components of many entheogens represent natural states of consciousness, and consuming them makes these radical states more available and predictable in their occurrence and duration.

Many entheogens produce chemicals that are naturally occurring in the brain.

Of course, we have the natural intuition that some representations of reality are more accurate than others. Dreaming consciousness is different from

from waking consciousness (though it is important to note that this is not assumed to be true in many cultures). Similarly, ordinary consciousness is closer to actual reality as it exists outside of our representations than one's consciousness under mushrooms. Nonetheless, both are ultimately con- structs of the mind. There are practical reason to believe this, and our culture is largely based on such presuppositions, but this supposition is not necessarily true from either a scientific or philosophical perspective. It is based on the unproven assumption that our "natural" perception is somehow a more fundamentally accurate and true representation of reality than are other states of consciousness.

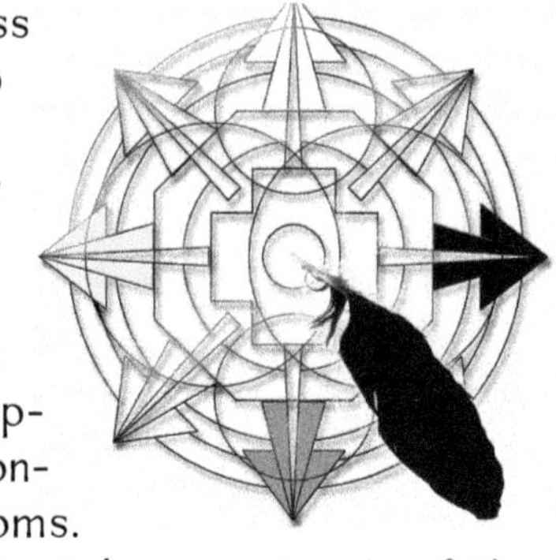

Another more useful view is that mushrooms are psychedelics. The word *psychedelic* means "mind-manifesting." Under this view, the implication is that what one experiences under the influence of mushrooms is actually manifestations of the mind. This may sound similar to the conclusion that mushrooms are hallucinogens in that the mind is certainly subjective and therefore not "objective" in the sense of representing reality accurately, but this is too crude. If we consider that all we ever experience is manifestations of our minds, in that our experience of reality is fundamentally a self-created representation, then the mind-manifesting powers of mushrooms take on a completely different implication.

"Objective" Reality

ENTHEOGENS, rather than simply distorting "reality," actually allow one to perceive more directly and more objectively how the mind engages in the process of reality construction. In other words, entheogens allow seekers to observe the processes of their mind. When under the influence of mushrooms, for example, mushroom eaters have an opportunity to watch how the mind processes information about the world and the self. Through the chemical interface of the body with the mushrooms, mushroom eaters are forced to re-orientate their sense of self to what they perceive through the sense organs and through the internal perception and experience of the mind, emotions, and body. What was previously habitual and second nature—normal construction of reality—becomes open to inspection, and deconstruction. In this state there are certainly experiences and impressions that may not conform to any direct sensory input from "outside," but that does not invalidate the experience as pure hallucination. It is just another construct of the mind, as is everything else.

The Witness is a state of consciousness where one can observe the contents of one's experience in a detached manner.

Thus the psychedelic experience is an experience of making the processes of the mind more open to observation and inspection. This is the opportunity of mushrooms, but it is not necessarily what one will experience. Truly observing the self constructing reality in the mushroom experience is different from simply going along for the psychedelic ride. What is crucial is to develop a sense of *The Witness*. The Witness is a state of consciousness where one can observe the contents of one's experience in a detached manner. In this state, mushroom eaters can observe their emotions, thoughts, and experiences without being attached to them. Only when one is in this state can one dispassionately observe the self's process of reality construction. This is the key to using mushrooms as a spiritual tool. Otherwise, seekers get caught in the mind-manifesting processes of the mushroom experience and get carried away by them. This can be both pleasant and disturbing, depending on the content and emotional resonance of the experience. Either way, it is not unlocking the potential of the mushrooms, however. To actually achieve the state of The Witness, it is perhaps best to think of mushrooms as plant teachers and as guides rather than as hallucinogens or psychedelics.

The key here is learning to distinguish between perceptions, interpretations, and the reactions to the sensory information received through the senses and the mind. As a tool of perception and cognition, entheogens allow users to observe the workings of the mind in radically new ways. Just as with any tool, it must be used correctly to produce productive and worthwhile results. A microscope, for example, is a great tool, when we know how to use it, what to look for, and what techniques to use to interpret the observations. By itself, a microscope only makes small objects appear larger. In the same way, entheogens make the workings of the mind more apparent and direct. The next step is learning how to make sense of the information that is garnered fr using the tool. As with all tools, ther are more effective and less effective ways of using entheogens and learning how to work with them for most productive results.

Chapter 3, Main Points:

* "Hallucination" implies that one's experience is fundamentally "not real." In contrast, when mushrooms are thought of as "mind-manifesting" psychedelics, we can see that mushrooms alter our perception of our minds and our patterns of reality construction.

* All of our sense of reality is a construction in our minds. It is a product of how we engage in the process of reality construction.

* Mushrooms open you up to the processes of your own mind. With mushrooms, it is possible to observe *how* you construct reality.

* Mushrooms are therefore a potent tool for introspection and self-discovery.

* The key for spiritual introspection is to become "The Witness," where you can observe yourself from a detached and objective vantage.

CHAPTER 4

Mushrooms as Plant Teachers

MY RELATIONSHIP TO MUSHROOMS moved closer to the indigenous, shamanic understanding of mushrooms and other *entheogens*—plants that evoke "god within"—when I truly experienced mushrooms as *teachers,* rather than as just hallucinogens or psychedelics. Various plants have been used for religion, healing, and spirituality around the world and throughout history. In indigenous contexts, sacred plants are understood to have the power to teach entheogen eaters essential knowledge and to bring them to states of divine consciousness. Every such entheogen-using culture has its own unique understanding and

> The archaic revival seeks cultural restoration of this lost symbiotic partner. It isn't ultimately a matter of the psychedelic experience per se: psilocybin has some unique relationship to the evolution of the human nervous system.
>
> -- Terence McKenna

> . . . it can be said that the growing interest in shamanism in general, and mushrooms in particular, represents part of a worldwide movement towards a more direct experiential and spiritual connection to the natural world.
>
> -- Ralph Metzner

system of practice and belief, but they all agree that the plants themselves are the teachers. These sacred plants are seen as genuine sources of knowledge for healing, health, wellbeing, spirituality, as well as profound ecological knowledge.

The tutelary nature of entheogens has largely been dismissed in the West, but this cultural prejudice is undergoing serious reconsideration. Many medicines used in the West had their origin in indigenous cultures. The indigenous consultants who have provided the most thorough and accurate ecological, pharmacological, and botanical information are entheogen-using shamans. Anthropologists attribute indigenous knowledge to generations of "trial and error," but the indigenous shamans disagree. Indigenous healers and shamans say that they learn their knowledge directly from the plants themselves. Where knowledge and use of entheogens have been preserved, the shamans are unequivocal that the sacred plants are the immediate source of their knowledge. The plants are their teachers.

When using mushrooms or other entheogens as spiritual tools, they become teachers. The mushrooms teach those who consume them. Seekers only need learn to listen to how they communicate and how they impart their lessons. This is the basis for using mushrooms with spiritual intent—being open to their lessons and their teachings.

Divine Essence?

THE TERM ENTHEOGENS WAS COINED by anthropologists and ethnobotanists to highlight how these sacred plants are understood in traditional cultures. Whether we believe there are "gods" or "God," or an "intelligence" within the mushroom experience or not is a personal choice and one all students of entheogens make for themselves. However, it is best, if simply for pragmatic purposes, to think of entheogens as teachers. If approached with the intention of letting them teach something and impart their wisdom, they will. Seekers cannot necessarily control what they teach, but they can choose to be open to their lessons.

Whether the mushrooms are just chemicals in the brain affecting the mind in a purely subjective manner or an actual communion with an alien or even divine intelligence with one's personal awareness is irrelevant when seekers take the experience as an opportunity to learn and choose to use the experience as a tool. The important thing is that seekers use it, and listen and pay attention to what is happening. Wise mushroom eaters are open to the lessons happening all around them all the time. They let the mushrooms guide them willingly and do it with perfect acceptance of all that they reveal.

The Lessons of Self

WHAT DO THE MUSHROOMS TEACH? Primarily, mushrooms teach about the self. At the very least, this is a natural starting place when using mushrooms and entheogens as spiritual tools. If they open seekers up to the process of their own mind and their means of reality construction, it is only natural the mushrooms teach seekers about *who and what they are*. This is meant in the broadest and most expansive sense. *The self* is not the ego-identified "me" of one's construction of reality. *The self* is a spiritual being that exists in the world of space and time. If the mushrooms teach seekers about the self, then they primarily teach about their spiritual nature as manifesting in space and time.

This is not to say that mushrooms only teach mushroom eaters about the spiritual self, but it is to say that this is the fundamental starting point for understanding how mushrooms can be used as spiritual tools. As experienced entheogens students will inform, these sacred plants also open students up to much more, opening up doors to other dimensions, radically other states of consciousness and being, and other intelligences.

However, the starting point of any genuine spiritual quest is with the self. If mushroom eaters don't understand their own nature, how could there be genuine understanding of anyone or anything else? True understanding begins with self-knowledge. Once we begin to understand the self, then we can begin to understand others and the universe in which we find ourselves. This is perhaps especially true for those coming from a Western culture where subjective states of the mind have been dismissed and the art of introspection and self-observation and contemplation has withered and atrophied to the state where we find ourselves meaningless machines in a meaningless world. In some sense, this could be seen as an urging for spiritual awakening, of accepting, experiencing, and

> True understanding begins with self-knowledge.

appreciating the role of Spirit and our spiritual natures as spiritual beings in a spiritual universe.

Everything about one's experience while under the influence of mushrooms is a learning opportunity.

Tutelary Spirits

IN MANY CULTURES the tutelary aspect of sacred plants is personified in the description of the "spirits" of plants that come to people and take them on shamanic journeys of discovery. People may experience this part of the mushroom journey differently, from spirits speaking to them, guiding them, and being "physically" present, to more of a disembodied sense of interacting with otherness or a guiding intelligence. The lessons are *always* there, however, and in the end it probably matters very little if the "spirit" of the mushroom takes on a solid or ephemeral form. Everything about the experience while under the influence of mushrooms is a learning opportunity.

Of course, this is always true and there is nothing unique about mushrooms or other entheogens in this sense. Spiritual seekers can always learn from their experience, no matter where they are or what conditions they find themselves in—and some would argue the more severe the conditions, the more opportunity for spiritual growth and learning. There are no limits or boundaries to spiritual experience or spiritual growth. The difference with mushrooms,

especially at stronger doses, is that this spiritual experience of self-reflection is more immediately accessible in a radical and visceral sense. It is therefore much easier to access information about how we construct our world and our sense of being under the influence of mushrooms. It provides the opportunity to observe the processes of one's own mind and therefore is a radical opportunity to learn about the self.

There are other methods for producing such states of consciousness. Many cultures and traditions have utilized a variety of means for generating altered states of consciousness. There is meditation, yoga, breathing techniques, ritual practices, sensory deprivation, fasting, physical exhaustion, and more. What is different about the use of entheogens is that in many respects they are more reliable, especially when used under the supervision of an experienced shaman. A practitioner can meditate for years and make little, if any. progress in achieving radical states of consciousness. Entheogens, on the other hand, produce radical effects. The true key is leaning how to use these effects productively and consciously. What is needed is the knowledge of how to absorb and make sense of the lessons that they impart.

Escapism or Spiritual Work

PERCEIVING AND APPRECIATING mushroom as teachers is not necessarily the natural state of the experience, at least not in our culture where sacred plants are lumped along side other mind-altering substances as "drugs," so that the tutelary aspect of the plants is often ignored, or even denied and denigrated. In cultures where the uses of sacred plants are respected and apprecied, a far different ethic and understanding is applied to the experience. For this reason, many people in our culture who use mushrooms do not necessarily approach them as teachers and as opportunities to learn. In fact, the opposite is probably more often true. Mushrooms are consumed for escape and fantasy, for the pure enjoyment of the experience and the aesthetic rapture that they can engender.

> Fear is a powerful force in that it convinces us to cling to our illusions and our deceptions because even if they make us miserable, at least they make us feel safe and secure.

People take mushrooms for enjoyment, and they certainly can be enjoyable. They can also be terrifying. When approached as teachers, however, the mushroom experience, while potentially profoundly joyful, and potentially radically difficult, is primarily *work*. Learning is work. Understanding our true self is work. Understanding the nature of the mind and our construction of reality is work. But it is work with profound rewards. To learn from mushrooms takes courage, dedication, and perseverance. They can be brutal teachers, for the truth is often hard to face. We wrap ourselves in so many illusions and self-generated lies that the mushrooms have to force us out of them to see the truth. This can be an extremely difficult and potentially harrowing process. It is not an experience that most people undertake willingly. Fear is a powerful force that convinces us to cling to our illusions and our deceptions because even when they make us miserable, at least they make us feel safe and secure.

In many respects, this is a deep pathology in contemporary Western culture—a refusal to look clearly and honestly at the darkness. We only need take a cursory glance at the proclaimed ideals of Western cultures and compare these ideals to the historical realities these noble ideals have produced to see that there is a deep, deep level of denial. Despite our claims of freedom and equality we have left a legacy of war, slavery, genocide, exploitation, and violence. In Western cultures, the shadow looms very large indeed.

Western cultures' denigration of entheogens is related to fear of The Shadow. That we live in a high state of denial and repression and fear is a major factor in our societies, from political policy to consumerism and advertising. We live in a deep state of fear and refusal to look honestly into the darkness of ourselves and seek to learn from what we find there. Cynically, this fear is widely manipulated in Western cultures, often to advantage of those in power. Fear keeps us obedient and passive to the powers that be. Do they have something to lose when people learn to free themselves from their fears and look honestly at reality?

Is it any wonder that the primary "drug" of choice in Western societies is alcohol, a drug that numbs the critical mind and the clear perceptions of our emotions and behaviors? For those who are unwilling or unable to look in the spiritual mirror, the deadening of thought, emotion, and awareness can be a blissful respite, even if it is fundamentally unhealthy, especially as those affected by alcohol tend to exacerbate unhealthy patterns and behaviors such as with violence, crime, and abuse.

To truly work with the spiritual nature of mushrooms and accept their spiritual lessons, seekers must free themselves from fear and be completely open to what they have to show, especially when looking into the darkness.

Chapter 4, Main Points:

* Mushrooms are natural teachers. When one is open to them, they will teach the spiritual seeker the lessons that need to be learned.

* Virtually all traditional cultures that use entheogens think of them as teachers.

* The first, and most important, subject to learn about in spiritual practice is one's self.

* Knowledge of self can then lead to knowledge of the world and of others.

* The lessons of mushrooms are often difficult. Most people are more comfortable and feel safer clinging to their illusions than facing the truth about themselves and their illusions.

* Fear is the force that causes us to cease to learn and get lost in the mushroom experience.

* Learning spiritual lessons from mushrooms is best understood as work.

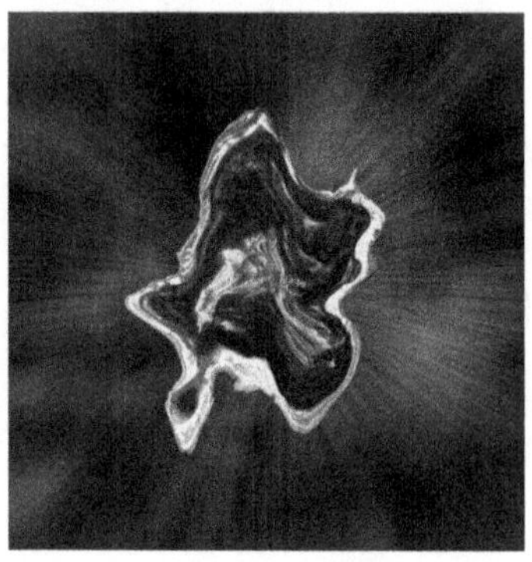

CHAPTER 5

Mushrooms as Spiritual Mirror

THE FUNDAMENTAL LESSON of mushrooms is that they serve as a spiritual mirror. They show seekers who they are and allow seekers to see themselves in all of their aspects in body, heart, mind, and spirit. The mushroom esperience penetrates through the surface of the seeker's illusions and masks to reveal the deeper core within.

The journey to one's inner core is often difficult and challenging. Few people truly want to look at themselves in the mirror. How many people can face themselves as they are, with all their strengths and weakness, all of their wounds, all of their masks, all of their ways of hiding from that which they don't want to see? We all carry

> . . . during the course of the experience I felt closer to my true self than I had ever been, more aware of my innermost feelings and thoughts.

shadows with us and there is darkness in all of us that keeps us from seeing the light on the far side of our illusions.

To accept the tutelage of the mushrooms is to accept the challenge to face our self in all of the lightness and darkness together. We are fundamentally whole beings and mushrooms reveal this to the spiritual seeker, but we've created so many illusions for ourselves that it is difficult to realize. Entheogens cut through the illusions like no other tool, if one lets them and learns to work with them.

Consciousness and Self-Deception

THE BURDEN OF CONSCIOUSNESS, of being and having awareness, is a heavy one. Life is hard. We are forced to make our way in the world with nothing but our own bodies, hearts, minds and spirits to guide us. This is a challenge like none other. It is not easy to be self-aware. We are alone in a vast universe with few protections from countless dangers and threats to our sense of self, safety, and well-being. We all struggle in our lives in countless ways. But the hardest thing is to be ourselves—that is our greatest challenge. Why? Because we have to be with ourselves all the time. Everything that we experience in the world is filtered through our own sense of self and being. We are the reality-constructors of our own experience. All that we know and experience is through ourselves and therefore everything we think we know is colored and influenced by our own sense of self.

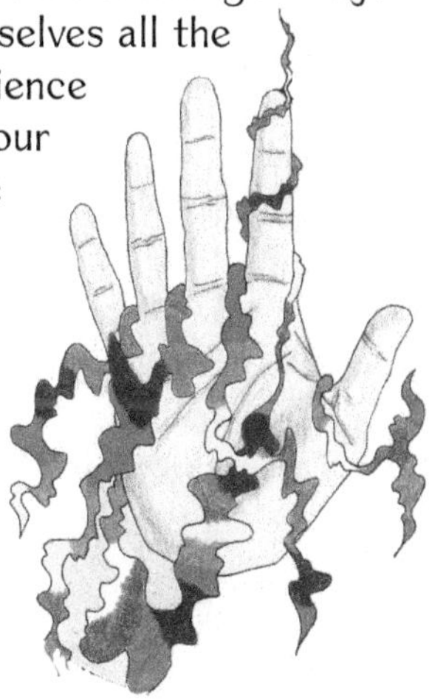

Most of the time we have a highly distorted view of

Who am I? is the pertinent question for any spiritual seeker.

ourselves. There are many aspects to this problem. From a philosophical perspective, we can see that we distort our perceptions of reality or what presumably exists "outside" of us through our concepts, our language, our belief systems, our cultures. But we also distort our reality-image of *ourselves* in countless ways, as we are also objects of our own perceptions and concepts. So not only do we distort information coming in from "outside," but we also distort our image of the very thing that is perceiving and experiencing the world. Is it any wonder we are filled with illusions and distortions? The key to unraveling our distortions and illusions is to understand the self. To understand the self, we have to understand how the self constructs its experience of reality.

Who Am I?

THERE ARE MANY WAYS that we answer this question. We give answers from our beliefs, from our views of ourselves and what we believe of reality. We may give a religious answer, or one that fits within our cultural framework. We may give an answer that reflects something we've read, or something we've learned in school. We may say something that others have said about us. We may give answers that reflect our social realities, our work, our families, our friendships. We may say something more personal that expresses what we believe about ourselves. Or we may give an answer that we know to be untrue, but we give it anyway because we want to believe it, or we want others to believe it. The more introspective one is, the more depth to the answer that will be given to this question.

Most of our answers fall into the category of conventional understanding. We repeat what we've learned or sincerely believe, but this does not mean that we honestly and truly understand ourselves. The difficult key to answering this question is the issue of honesty. Can we be honest with ourselves? Can we accept ourselves as we are without judgment or self-criticism? Can we embrace our darker and more negative aspects of our being? The true challenge is to face our darkness and embrace it, and thereby pass through it. This is precisely the task that most people are deathly fearful of. To engage in such an introspective process is to open ourselves up to all of our wounds, our judgments, our abuses, of both ourselves and others, our petty emotional attachments, and our convenient lies that we tell ourselves about who and what we are. But we must be willing to look at these aspects of the self if we are to come to see the deeper unity and wholeness.

The true challenge is to embrace our darker and more negative aspects of our being and to thereby pass through them.

Facing the Darkness

A FUNDAMENTAL STARTING POINT to spiritual work is knowing that we all have darkness and aspects about ourselves, our behavior and our beliefs that we are not happy with. While perhaps a negative view, it is fairly easy to see this in ourselves and in others. When faced with the reality of who and what we are, most people are terrified—and rightly so. We've spent our entire lives covering over our wounds and denying the parts of ourselves we don't like, or have been taught not to like. We wear our faces like masks that project what we want to be and desperately try to cover what we don't want others to see. Who then, is ready to look in the spiritual mirror and have all these truths presented to oneself. It is a challenge beyond all others and perhaps the most difficult thing that we can possibly do.

Why? Because we judge ourselves constantly. We tell ourselves that we should be this way or that way. We're not good enough. We're not smart enough. We have the wrong thoughts or the wrong feelings. We make mistakes and we judge ourselves for it. This causes tremendous mental and emotional pain and because it hurts so much, we cover it over and pretend that it doesn't exist. Our most common solution is to repress, deny, or mask. This is our natural state of dealing with our self-perception.

The Mirror of Others

HOW CAN WE KNOW OURSELVES? A good place for spiritual seekers to start is to consider how they treat and react to others. How we treat others is a mirror of how we treat ourselves. If we are quick to judge others, then we are quick to judge ourselves. If we are impatient with others, we are impatient with ourselves. If we are critical and abusive of others, we are critical and abusive of ourselves.

How often have you seen someone behaving in a way that made you feel embarrassed, even though the behavior was not your own? How often have you gotten unduly aggravated by another's behavior that somehow got under your skin, even though no one else seems to have minded? How often have you felt bad about yourself and you've passed on that sense of criticism and failure to others, telling them they're stupid, not worthy, or a failure?

> Everywhere we turn there are mirrors, showing us who we are and how we behave and think, but we do everything we can to project it outwards, away from ourselves.

Good or bad, this is our natural way of acting and behaving. We treat others as we treat ourselves. We think of others as we think of ourselves. The trouble is that most of us have seriously distorted and negative views ourselves that we then project onto others, or are forced to confront in ourselves when we see it in them.

Think of the person you dislike the most or who grates on you in ways that might seem irrational. What do you have in common with this person? Are you reminded of yourself? Chances are, you have far more in common with this person than you want to admit. Or perhaps your dislike comes from jealousy. Maybe this person is good at something that you are severely critical of in yourself.

Everywhere we turn there are mirrors, showing us who we are and how we behave and think, but we do everything we can to project this reflection outwards, away from ourselves. Most people don't want to take an honest look in that mirror and see what it truly and honestly reveals to them.

Facing the Spiritual Mirror

FACING THE SPIRITUAL MIRROR is perhaps the most difficult thing we can ever do. If doing this is so hard in everyday life, imagine how difficult it can be when under the influence of mushrooms. The greater the challenge, the greater the reward and the deeper the insights gained. Only by facing our demons—and this can take on a quite literal meaning with mushrooms—can we come to embrace the self as it actually is, not as one has carefully projected it to be.

These insights are not new. Most readers of these pages have an understanding of the process

When you meet someone who is free from these illusions and abuses, you know it. There is a sense of peace and pure sincerity and integrity about that person.

of projection, repression, denial, and self-criticism. Much of our culture's system of therapy is designed to confront and overcome these aspects of ourselves. We have technical and layperson terms to refer to these psychological processes and evidence of their truth is all around us all the time. How many gay-bashers deny their own homosexual feelings? How many politicians who rail against pornography have a secret stash of porn locked away? How many people trying desperately to convert you to their religion or way of belief are filled with doubts and insecurities? How many people feel better about themselves when putting others down and criticizing them?

Sadly, the numbers are far too many. In many respects, this seems to be our natural state. It is not, however, our necessary state. It is how we act when we are wrapped in illusions and self-deceptions. If we are at peace with ourselves, why criticize others? If we can accept ourselves, then why would we try and change others? If we are comfortable with our own behavior, why would we try and change the behavior of others? If we are confident and firm in our own views, why would we always try and convince others that we're right and they're wrong?

Perhaps you've met someone who isn't this way and perhaps this person has made an impression on you. There are people who do not seem to be wrapped in fear and illusion. They might be naturally more open and accepting of themselves, or they may have strived and struggled with difficult spiritual practice. But when you meet someone who is free from illusions and these abuses, you know it. There is a sense of peace and pure sincerity and integrity about that person. That person does not need to judge others. That person does not need to convince you of anything. And that person accepts you for who you are without judgment. Such people are gifts and we should be thankful when their paths cross our own.

> Mushrooms can bring the spiritual seeker right to the heart and root of his personal issues, especially if used consciously with spiritual intent and purpose.

In theory, anyone can be such a person, rich in spiritual awareness and conscious of the traps and illusions of the human mind. In reality, to achieve such a state of being takes practice, dedication, and a great deal of work, and that work must start with the self. The key for spiritual seekers is facing their self and accepting what they find without judgment, illusion, or criticism. This is far easier said than done, and perfecting it could take a lifetime and beyond.

The Psychedelic Path

SOME PEOPLE WORK WITH THERAPISTS for years to overcome these difficulties and to find acceptance and peace within themselves. Others spend years in intense dedication to a religious or spiritual practice trying to seek some resolution. Others drown out their fears, criticisms, and projections with addictions of all kinds from drugs to religion and politics. Others turn to black and white dogma to assure themselves that they are right and saved, if only they can do X, Y, and Z.

But imagine—what if we could perform the most profound spiritual work in one evening, achieving deep spiritual insights that can serve as nourishment for further contemplation and spiritual work for years

to come, even a lifetime? Even one encounter with psilocybin mushrooms or another entheogen can transform a person's life and perspectives of self, world, and others. Mushrooms can bring spiritual seekers right to the heart and root of their personal issues, especially if they are used consciously with spiritual intent and purpose. Perhaps the seeker won't get to the very core all at once, for most of our illusions and wounds are complex with multiple layers and aspects to them, but mushrooms *will* show seekers what they need to see and they *will* give seekers the opportunity to face themselves, often whether it is desired or not, and in doing so, they hold the power within them to make a profound and lasting impact that can cleanse a person's body, heart, mind, and spirit.

Good Trip/Bad Trip

MOST PEOPLE UNDERSTAND the psychedelic experience to divide into two basic categories: the "good" trip, and the "bad" trip. Much has been written about how to have a "good" trip with psychedelics and how to avoid a "bad" trip. Most often the advice centers around the concepts of set and setting. The advice is that "trippers" should be aware of their mindset when entering into the experience. Is the person depressed, happy, overly concerned about something, have pressing issues on his or her mind? Secondly, is the setting conducive to a good experience? Is the person comfortable with the other trippers? Is the person in a safe and secure environment so as to not feel endangered or exposed?

These are certainly important considerations and one would be foolish to ignore them. However, this is really just advice for having a "good" trip and avoiding a "bad" one. It is not advice for using mushrooms as a spiritual tool. Under the set and setting model, it is not difficult to see that a "good" trip is one where seekes don't feel challenged or confronted, so that they feel safe and secure. The person is with friends or in a comfortable environment and feels safe enough to enjoy the aesthetic and psychedelic aspects of the experience. Seekers might have intricate visions or beautiful, dreamy thoughts and images that float through their minds. But what are they really doing? They are enjoying themselves—they are "tripping," and "digging" it. There isn't anything necessarily wrong with this, but they are certainly not using mushrooms the way they can be used and they are not getting from the experience the most valuable of lessons.

When using mushrooms as a spiritual mirror, one comes out of the experience with a deep and profound sense of realization and understanding about oneself and the world that is created by the mind.

On the other side is the "bad" trip. Bad trips are where seekers are fearful and fight against the flow of the mushrooms. The environment is uncomfortable; the people are wrong. Seekers feel judged and judge themselves, so they try to stop the experience, but can't. In fact, the more they fight, the worse it becomes as they are beset by demons and hellish nightmare images that they wish desperately to escape.

Ultimately, both experiences are two sides of the same coin. The "good" trip reaffirms the seeker's sense of self. The seeker is with people who don't challenge one and is in an environment that comfortable and relaxing. Al seeker is doing is reaffirming positive illusions. Similarly, on the "bad" trip, the seeker is being confronted by negative illusions and judgments, but gives them power by fighting against them. The primary instinct is to escape, to return to safe illusions, but if the trip is bad enough, seekers don't know how to get back to the realm of safety, and they suffer.

The Transcendent Journey

NEITHER USE OF MUSHROOMS is particularly useful from the *Mushroom Wisdom* perspective. There is plenty of opportunity to learn in these experiences, but it is difficult without approaching the experience with the proper mindset. Those who have such experiences come away with "Wow—that was beautiful and amazing," or "That was one hellish nightmare that I don't ever want to return to again!" The difference is that when using mushrooms as a spiritual mirror, seekers come out of the experience with a deep and profound sense of realization and understanding about their self and the world that is created by the mind. They emerge from the experience fundamentally changed by it, and this is the healthiest and most beneficial change possible. This is the difference between enjoying a psychedelic playground and engaging in true spiritual work that has the power to be profoundly transformative, where seekers can transcend the normal boundaries of self, world, and being and come out of the journey with wisdom, humility, and ultimately joy and acceptance.

Sadly, it is often far easier for us to hold onto illusions, even painful and negative ones, than it is to face the truth honestly and with integrity and transcend our limiting judgments and perspective.

Looking into the spiritual mirror is not easy. Most people spend their entire lives trying desperately *not* to look into the mirror, fearful of what they will find therein. To look in the spiritual mirror we must directly face all the negative things we don't like and fully embrace all of our emotional wounds. We have to be willing to give up our protective masks. And most difficult of all, *we have to be honest*. Being honest with oneself is probably the most difficult of challenges because it means looking carefully and without judgment at who and what we are. But we are so full of judgment and criticism that we rarely have the genuine opportunity to be honest, because as soon as we face something negative, we judge it, and ourselves. We beat ourselves up constantly in our darkest moments as we inflict endless amounts of abuse on ourselves. Sadly, it is often far easier to hold onto illusions, even painful and negative ones, than it is to face the truth honestly and with integrity and transcend our limiting judgments and perspective. The transcendent journey is the spiritual path that leads out of these illusions, judgments, and self-inflicted pain and suffering.

Working with mushrooms as spiritual mirrors is not about a "good" or a "bad" trip. It is about work, perseverance, honesty, and a willingness to confront and embrace the darkness. That is the key to finding the light, peace, and acceptance that waits on the other side. To get there, seekers *must* be willing to work through the darkness. And by working through the darkness I do not mean banishing it. On the contrary, I mean embracing it and accepting it without judgment or emotional attachment, either positive or negative. If we do this work—whether with entheogens or any other spiritual path—*it will change our life.* How much it will change our life depends on us as individual's and how far we are willing to go.

As spiritual beings, it is our right to take up the challenge. The remainder of this book will be a careful study of how mushrooms contribute to this difficult, but immensely rewarding task of looking in the spiritual mirror, passing through the darkness, and finding the bright light of wisdom on the far side.

Chapter 5, Main Points:

* Working with mushrooms is *looking into the spiritual mirror.*

* The spiritual mirror shows us as we really are.

* While any environment and any context can be a spiritual mirror, this ability to look in the spiritual mirror is greatly enhanced by mushrooms.

* Looking in the spiritual mirror is not about a "good" or "bad" trip. It is about facing one's self with honesty and integrity to recover the authentic self.

* Most people are deathly afraid of looking into the spiritual mirror.

* Living with illusions, pain, and deceit is often perceived as being easier than looking at oneself honestly.

* Looking in the spiritual mirror requires dedication and a willingness to work.

CHAPTER 6

The Witness

IN OUR NORMAL, EVERYDAY CONSCIOUSNESS, we identify so closely with our constructs and illusions and the emotions that are integral to them that we accept the illusions for reality, when in fact they are not. We become attached to our thoughts and feelings and believe that they define our essential nature and identity.

> . . . psilocybin can produce a state of dissociation or detachment from the roles and games of everyday interaction. This detachment, or temporary suspension of defenses, can provide insight and perspective about repetitive behavior or thought patterns and open up the way for the construction of alternatives.
>
> -- Timothy Leary

This is true for both positive and negative emotions and thoughts. When we are happy, we say, "I'm happy." When we're sad, we say, "I'm sad." And our attachments to these emotions and thoughts color the way that we construct the reality of the world around us. When we are happy, the world seems to be happy with us. Small things bring us joy and the world takes on a positive light. Oppositely, when we are sad, the world is a dark and depressing place. Positive or negative, we develop attachments to our thoughts and emotions and use them to construct our reality.

Mushroom Consciousness

IN THE STRANGE FLUX OF THE MUSHROOM EXPERIENCE, these qualities of consciousness and the process of the construction of reality can be presented to spiritual seekers in the most profound way. Given the nature of mushrooms, the mushroom eater can easily get carried away by thoughts and emotions. When this happens in a negative sense, the trip becomes "bad." Attachment to emotions and the thoughts that go with them can be so powerful that the mushroom eater is overwhelmed by them. This can also happen with positive thoughts and emotions, and the mushroom eater tends to think of this positively as it makes for an enjoyable and pleasant trip. Neither is using mushrooms spiritually, however.

When in the mushroom experience, and ideally, at all times of one's life, spiritual seekers can adopt the perspective of "The Witness." Most of the time we are so caught up in our illusions, projections, and self-deceptions that we take our experience, our emotions, and our state of mind as ourselves. We identify with the thoughts and emotions and think "This is me. This is how I experience myself and the world." This is an illusion, at least in some very important respects. When one attains the state of The

> When one attains the state of The Witness, this illusory nature of everyday consciousness and our self-identifying constructs becomes immediately obvious.

Witness, this illusory nature of everyday consciousness and our self-identifying constructs becomes immediately obvious. This is the first, and perhaps most important, key to working with mushrooms to develop spiritual consciousness, and indeed, is generally crucial for any form of spiritual practice. Appearances should not be taken for reality.

Transcendent Awareness

COUNTLESS RELIGIOUS TRADITIONS, especially those more open to introspection and the cultivation of mystical awareness, emphasize the view that our "true self" is not our ego-identified sense of self. Christian mystics talk about the purity of the soul and direct union with the Godhead, the foundation of all reality behind appearances and conventions. Buddhist mystics speak of "no-self" and "no-mind," and the cultivation of awareness that transcends ordinary conceptual consciousness and oneness with the Buddha Mind. Hindus speak of the Atman, the true self that is identical to God and is not bound by any limits of thought or conception, being without form, without distinction between self and other. There are as many ways of describing such forms of awareness as there are religions, or even more realistically, there are as many possible descriptions as there are people who attain transcendent states of awareness.

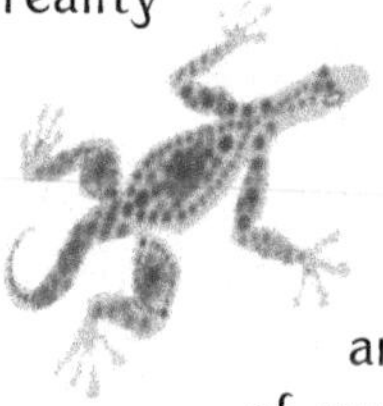

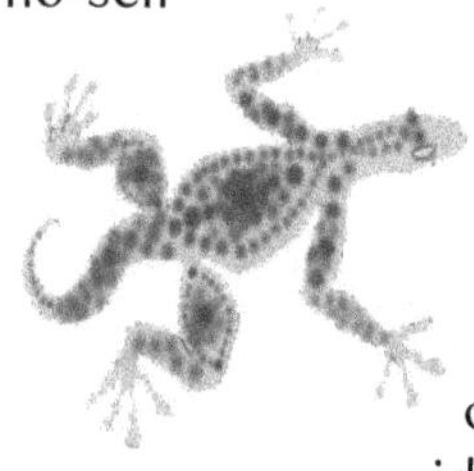

Part of the difficulty of describing transcendent states of awareness is that any communication of such a state must take place in terms available to ordinary consciousness. Language, concepts, conventions, metaphors, images, and symbols must all be used to express something that is ultimately ineffable—something that is not amenable to ordinary methods of expression or communication. There simply are no words that can accurately express the direct experience of transcendental awareness, which is why so many mystics speak of nothingness, emptiness, God without form, total union of subject and object, and the disintegration of ego-identified sense of self and being. Something so radical cannot be captured by language. It can only be experienced to be truly appreciated and known as the radical mystery that it is.

> We can choose to feel or think what we want, and we can choose how and who we want to be.

Seeing Through the Eyes of the Witness

WHILE THE EXPERIENCE OF THE WITNESS and the achievement of full mystical enlightenment are not necessary identical, they do share a great deal in common in that the experience of The Witness provides the opportunity to transcend normal, limiting aspects of conscious awareness, and this has a profound effect on one's sense of self, being, and spiritual identity.

Imagine being able to observe and explore your emotions and thoughts without being attached to them. When we are attached to our emotions and thoughts, we pass judgment on them. "I want to feel this way." "I should be like this." "I shouldn't be like this." "I hate feeling this way." We accept our judgments as reality, when they are only our judgments. We think about what we should and shouldn't feel, the way we should and shouldn't be, the thoughts we should and shouldn't think. We judge ourselves constantly and we project these judgments out into the world about us and onto other people and things. We think of ourselves as happy, or as being in pain, or as suffering, or as being superior, or unworthy. We do this all the time of every day.

What we don't often realize is that all of this is based on our choices. We can choose to feel or think what we want, and we can choose how and who we want to be. It is our ingrained beliefs and attachments that limit our choices, often to the point that we forget that we have a choice and that the emotions and thoughts we are experiencing may be based on illusions, judgments, and criticisms.

Who hasn't asked the question, "Why do I always do X?" At some point, everyone confronts themselves with such critical questioning. We present the question to ourselves as if we have a choice—and we do. But chances are, even when we ask this question, we've already rationalized the behavior and emotions to ourselves and we think that they are inevitable. Though we'd like to exert choice over the situation, we convince ourselves that we can't, and we say, "I guess I really am just that way." We accept our own self-limiting thoughts and judgments and then treat them as though they are reality. We identify so closely with our thoughts and emotions and the illusions that they help create that we can't find a perspective from outside of them that clearly and easily tells us, "It doesn't have to be that way."

This is the perspective of The Witness. It is quite a strange and wonderful state to be in. Imagine being able to fully explore all of your thoughts, emotions, illusions, criticisms, and judgments so that you can understand and appreciate them, but not be attached to them. This is the perspective of The Witness. The Witness sees and experiences, but does not become attached to anything either good or bad, positive or negative, beautiful or ugly. From the perspective of The Witness, one can take in anything and appreciate it for what it is without being caught in the trap of attachment or judgment.

The Nature of the Witness

WHAT IS THE WITNESS? According to one's beliefs, religious views, or culture or tradition, different spiritual seekers will give a different answer to this question. Some may feel the need to attach a particular ontological status to The Witness, which may or may not be in agreement with the understanding of other spiritual seekers. Ultimately, it probably matters very little what the reality status of The Witness is or what kind of name one might give it. The most important thing is not *what* The Witness is, but rather that it *can* be experienced and that to experience it is profoundly transformative and beneficial.

It is the perspective of The Witness that allows the spiritual seeker to look into the spiritual mirror with honesty and integrity. Anything less is to look into the mirror still caught in one's illusions, judgments, and projections. Looking into the spiritual mirror through the constructs of ego-identity is looking into the mirror while wearing a mask. The Witness has no need to wear a mask or make judgments. All that The Witness does is what its name implies—it witnesses, and that is all.

Looking into the spiritual mirror through the constructs of ego-identity is looking into the mirror while wearing a mask.

The Witness allows us, at least in some degree, to experience our true nature. As self-aware beings, we are fundamentally pure consciousness. What we identify as ourselves, that thing we call "I" or "me" is a collection of patterns manifesting in space-time. We attach emotions and judgments onto this process of manifestation and through it come to identify what we think of as ourselves. A strange thing happens when observing oneself from the perspective of The Witness, however. These patterns that we identify with are seen as just that—patterns manifesting in space-time, but the fact that they are not our true nature or self becomes immediately obvious and self-evident. These are illusions at play in the field of manifestation. At the core, we are pure, whole, and undivided consciousness, or *spirit*. It is The Witness that connects us back to the source. From this perspective we can see that we do have thoughts, feelings, emotions, judgments, and so forth, but they are not necessarily who we are in a fundamental sense. We make choices to identify with these things, but our essential nature is something much deeper.

How we choose to construct reality has a profound effect on what we experience and how we think of ourselves and others.

The Dream of Reality

IN AN ORDINARY DREAM, we experience ourselves as a self-identified being among others in situations outside of our control or direct influence, much like normal reality with some possible strangeness due to it being a dream. Generally, we are not aware that we are dreaming and simply accept what we experience as "reality" and act accordingly.

However, it is entirely possible to "wake up" within a dream, which is called "lucid" dreaming. When this happens, the dream becomes profoundly different. When we know that we are dreaming, we know that we have far more control over our experience than we are normally aware of. You can actually watch as your thoughts and emotions change the content and experience of the dream. You realize that everything you perceive is altered by your own thoughts, emotions, and judgments. You are the master of your dream and you can change it at will. If you don't like something in the dream, you can simply change it. What a profound gift to wake up in this way! If only everything were so easy.

In essence, everything is open to such profound change and control, at least in some very important respects. Reality, as we experience it (which is the only reality we will ever know), is a construction of our minds, just as is a dream. This is not to say that "you are all just figments of my imagination—you are just characters in my dream of reality," but it is to say that how we choose to construct reality has a profound effect on what we experience and how we think of ourselves and others.

We are making choices about how we want our reality to be all the time, but most of the time, just like the blissful dreamer, we are unaware of how our choices, thoughts, and judgments are affecting our experience of reality, so much so that we think that reality is something that is *happening to us* rather than something that we are *actively constructing* every moment of every day. The waking world is far more complicated than the dreaming world, but only for the fact that the waking world is shared with so many

The Witness allows spiritual seekers to wake up to their own dream of reality. From this perspective, spiritual seekers can actually take a look at how they are creating their reality.

other beings who all bring their own personal dream to the collective. We each do our part in creating reality, however, and everything we experience of ourselves and the world is filtered through our own sense of self and being, so the comparison to a dream is far more relevant than it might seem at first.

Awakening to the Dreaming

THE WITNESS ALLOWS SPIRITUAL SEEKERS to wake up to their own dream of reality. From this perspective, spiritual seekers can actually take a look at how they are creating their reality. The Witness helps them to look at themselves and their process of creating reality from a detached and dispassionate perspective.

When looking from the perspective of the Witness, seekers can actually observe their ego-identified selves from a perspective that is not caught in that ego-identity. The seeker can look in the spiritual mirror through the eyes of The Witness and neither judge nor reject what is seen therein. One can simply, truthfully, and honestly see the contents of the mirror what for they are.

The Witness always knows what that spiritual seeker has to see in the mirror, what lessons need to be learned, what insights gained. Often, this aspect of The Witness almost takes on a quality of otherness, as though one is being shown elements of his or her life by a knowledgeable force that exists beyond the self. It is as though all one's history is made available to an impartial observer who will help the spiritual seeker through the difficult process of seeing his or her life in all its aspects.

Perhaps the greatest gift of The Witness is that through it, the spiritual seeker can look into one's own heart. One's heart, and the emotions and judgments

The heart is the doorway to the light of Spirit beyond. It is the doorway to one's source.

that every person carries within it, is the substance of what is revealed in the spiritual mirror. When one looks into the spiritual mirror, one *must* look into one's own heart. The heart is the doorway to the light of Spirit beyond. It is the doorway to one's source. When one's heart is clean, Spirit can flow through openly and unimpeded, like a pure wind through an open door. The work of looking into the spiritual mirror is the work of cleaning out one's own heart. That is the work of The Witness.

Awareness Without Judgment

WHEN WE SEE OURSELVES in the spiritual mirror, we look without judgment and attachment. This is what allows us to look into our hearts. Due to our self-judgments and our attachments to our illusions, our hearts can become filled with wounds and suffering. This is the source of our darkness and our fears. This is what people who don't want to look into the spiritual mirror don't want to see. The pain is too great. The demons are too strong. It is too hard to face the truth that we carry in our hearts.

Our hearts always know the truth. They carry the history of our actions and our judgments that we pass upon ourselves within them. We spend most of our lives trying to cover over the pain in our hearts, but without addressing it, it only becomes stronger and the patterns that created it in the first place only take a stronger hold. We deny, we repress, we sublimate, we create illusions and masks and we hang on to them as if our lives depended on them, because we are too afraid to look into our hearts and deal with what we may find there.

But to look through the eyes of The Witness is to look with eyes that have no fear. When we can look at our heart without attachment or judgment, we can learn from what we find there. And the lessons that we learn will be the key to the healing that will come. As spiritual seekers, we can heal our heart. We can clean it out. But to clean it out, we must be willing to look into it with honesty and integrity.

The Witness is therefore the spiritual seeker's Ally. The Witness shows the seeker what needs to be seen, what needs to be acknowledged, what needs to be made peace with. The spiritual seeker's Ally will walk us to the precipice of our own darkness so that we can learn from it and embrace it. The spiritual seeker's Ally helps us to face our fear and let it pass through us unharmed. The seeker's Ally teachs us to be a spiritual alchemist. Spiritual seekers can take the fear, the pain, the wounds, the judgment, the criticism, and can turn it into knowledge that will empower them—but it takes work.

Chapter 6, Main Points:

* One's heart and the emotions that one carries within it is the substance of the spiritual mirror. When one looks into the spiritual mirror, one must look into one's own heart. The heart is the doorway to the light of Spirit beyond.

* When the heart is clean, spirit can flow through openly and unimpeded, like a pure wind through an open door.

* Our hearts always know the truth. They carry the history of our actions and our judgments that we pass upon ourselves within them.

* To look through the eyes of The Witness is to look with eyes that have no fear.

* Honestly facing our fears and wounds is transformative. It empowers us and is the source of self-healing.

CHAPTER 7

Patterns

IF THERE IS JUST ONE THING that even a passing experience with mushroom will teach any mushroom eater, it is that the basic nature of phenomenal reality is an ongoing expression of countless interconnected patterns. Everything that exists in phenomenal reality is caught in the flux of space-time. Everything is flowing and changing all the time. Everything that manifests in space-time occurs through the manifestation of patterns, including our experience of reality. Patterns go all the way "up" and all the way "down." From sub-atomic particles to galaxies and

> [with mushrooms there is]. .. enhancement of all sensory modalities, synaesthesias, brightly colored kaleidoscopic visuals behind closed eyelids, perception of interconnected webs and lattices of energy patterns that seem to be full of spiritual and psychological meaning as well a visually gorgeous.
>
> -- Ralph Metzner

universes, everything is made of patterns. Absolutely everything that exists is made of patterns, including our conscious awareness of self and the world.

One does not need to eat mushrooms to accept the basic truth of the above premise. Take a look around you. Is there anything you can identify that is not part of a pattern, or more accurately, countless numbers of interconnecting and interpenetrating embedded hierarchies of patterns?

Most science is based on recognition of patterns. Take the work of physicists, for example. They see patterns of energy that they give different names like superstrings, quarks, electrons, photons, and atoms, but these are all names for patterns of energy and light that manifest in space-time and construct what physicists refer to as the physical world.

For the most part, when discussing the world of the very very small, physicists tell us that objects as we understand them do not exist. There are patterns of probability that extend from the past through the present and into the future, which is mathematically described by the quantum wave function. When physicists try to isolate an "object," they largely can't. For example, it is impossible to discuss quantum physics in terms of objects, as least as we conventionally understand them.

Physicists speak of vibrations and patterns of wave/particle energy. Try to turn a sub-atomic "particle" into an object and you lose precious information. You can either assign a sub-atomic "particle" a definite place in space, or a particular momentum, but not both at the same time. Imagine if someone told you that they could either tell you where a car was, or how fast it was going, but that it was impossible to tell you both at the same time! As physicists understand it, this is how the sub-atomic world works. Patterns cannot be isolated into discrete objects, for doing so loses sight of the vibratory well of possibility that manifests as an object.

Going deeper than the sub-atomic is the strange world of superstrings. Here physicists claim that what are taken to be sub-atomic particles are more accurately understood as vibrations of multi-dimensional "strings" that are the vibratory substrate from which other patterns of energy that manifest in space-time emerge. From this perspective, everything we experience has its source in the fundamental vibrations of superstrings. All of existence is like a grand symphony of vibrating strings. As a metaphor, one might claim that reality is made of music, and what is music if not patterns of vibration and resonance manifesting in space-time?

> What we perceive and describe as the "physical" world is an intricate system of patterns embedded within patterns within patterns within patterns.

Returning to the world of macro-sized objects, one can easily perceive that all of nature is based on patterns of manifestation. From a common sense perspective, it is easy to see that physical objects are all caught in various biological and physical patterns of growth, development, and decay, from living beings to planets and galaxies. However, there are more precise ways that scientists have sought to describe the patterned nature of reality beyond the descriptions of say biology, geology, and astronomy. The mathematical systems of fractals and chaos theory have been developed in recent years to map out and describe the processes through which physical objects develop. Fractal mathematics can be used to analyze the development of shapes of clouds, branches of trees, river courses, shorelines, fern leaves, and the formation of galaxies and astronomical phenomena.

What we perceive and describe as the "physical" world is an intricate system of patterns embedded within patterns within patterns within patterns. In this sense, patterns go all the way "up" to the largest physical objects that we know of as well as all the way "down" to the smallest of sub-atomic particles and beyond. There is nothing in the physical world that we cannot describe as part of a pattern, or many overlapping patterns.

Patterns Within Patterns

DEPENDING ON THE LEVEL OF OUR INVESTIGATION into objects, we find different patterns and different connections to other objects and different patterns. For example, we can describe a tree as a collection of sub-atomic particles, a fractal pattern, a growing thing that responds to patterns of light, temperature, and water, and the intrinsic life-cycle of the plant and its genetic structure, which is itself a pattern of coded information that gives the blue-print for the patterned development of the living thing. There are multiple hierarchies of interconnecting patterns, which, when fully appreciated, makes the isolation of fundamentally separate objects difficult to justify.

In philosophy, analyzing the world in this manner is called the study of "systems" or "systems theory." Everything is seen as systems of interaction where the whole is greater than the sum of its parts. Even a simple tree is a collection of many different systems of interaction from the smallest to the largest scale. What binds it all together is patterns.

In Buddhist philosophy this is called "inter-connectedness," or "co-dependent origination," and is a fundamental teaching of the Buddha. The nature of interconnectedness is represented by the "jeweled net of Indra," where each jewel in the net reflects every other jewel. Every apparently discrete object is fundamentally connected to every other object. Within this system, there is only the appearance of relative isolation, but when looked at from a larger perspective, all sense of separateness is fundamentally an illusion.

Everything is made of patterns. They're everywhere, all the time.

Everything is made of patterns. They're everywhere, all the time. What a fantastic world to live in! Everything is changing all the time. Every moment of existence is a further expression of countless, innumerable, intertwined and interconnecting patterns and systems of manifestation. This is the great flux of existence, the manifestation of patterns in space-time. Everything in the universe is in constant movement and change according to defining patterns that give the shape, form, and expression to everything we experience. The phenomenal world is fundamentally one of change. Patterns that are more stable and enduring we tend to call objects. Other, less obvious and less stable patterns we might think of as processes. But everything is made of patterns, which is the fundamental nature of how things exist.

Caught in the Flux

YOU AND I, as self-aware and conscious beings in this ever-changing flux of space-time, are no different. We, too, are patterns, all the way "up" and all the way "down," from every aspect of our physical nature to our mental, emotional, and spiritual natures. We construct our own experience of reality through patterns, just like everything else. We have patterns of thought, patterns of belief, patterns of emotional reactions, patterns of perception, patterns of behavior, patterns of choices and decisions. We are a profound collection of interconnected patterns manifesting through the constantly changing world of space-time.

We are a profound collection of interconnected patterns manifesting through the constantly changing world of space-time.

This is our fundamental state of being in the phenomenal world. While mystical traditions proclaim that it is possible to transcend our limited experience of space-time, or manifest reality, in that state there is complete absorption with the source of being, which lies beyond the flux of phenomenal space-time. Thus the source of being may be fundamentally unchanging, but everything we experience in our phenomenal existence is in a constant state of change, ourselves included. While it would be nice if we could all go directly to the source, that is a goal that very few will ever achieve. We have to struggle with our own manifesting patterns in space-time every moment of our existence. It is the rare and blessed person who can easily transcend this quality of our existence.

Mushrooms help the spiritual seeker to perceive, understand, and make peace with the patterns that govern his or her own particular manifestation in the world. The more one understands this process, the closer one comes to understanding and experiencing the source of being. It is a long and difficult road, however, and most people will never reach the end, if there is an end, but the very act of striving can make profound differences in one's life and one's understanding of who and what one is.

Creatures of Habit

HUMANS ARE CREATURES OF HABIT. This is not only true, but also largely necessary for us to have any understanding of our experience. We have to learn how to make sense of our experience and the things that we encounter in our world. Through our concepts, languages, beliefs, traditions, and cultures, we learn to organize our experience into things that we can presumably know and understand. A large part of childhood is learning how to structure our experience of reality into things that we can identify and comprehend. We divide the world into objects and concepts, truths and untruths, things that are correct and things that are incorrect, things that are right and wrong. We learn all of this through patterns of thought and behavior. We learn ways of thinking, acting, and feeling. These become our habits, our ways of constructing our reality.

When one starts to think of the self as a collection of patterns, it is easy to see these collections of patterns everywhere. We have daily patterns that we follow. We have certain patterns of thought that we continually follow. We have certain patterns of emotional reactions. We have patterns of behavior. We have patterns of speaking. We have patterns of making decisions and approaching choices. We have patterns for how we carry and hold our bodies. We are made of patterns.

Most of the time these patterns tend to run on "automatic pilot" in the sense that we do not consciously think them through. We just are the patterns. They are what make us who we are and we don't put a great deal of thought into them unless something comes along that presents a challenge to our patterns or we

Patterns tend to run on "automatic pilot" in the sense that we do not consciously think them through.

Humans, as patterned beings, will do everything that we can to fit our experience into our pre-existing patterns, even if those patterns are unhealthy and harmful to us.

encounter a situation where our patterns cause us emotional distress.

At that point, we may come to question our patterns, but this is actually rather rare, because reactions to disturbances are patterns as well. When one of our patterns causes us emotional distress, the most common reaction is to be defensive, to shift blame, and to judge ourselves, or others. This process starts another cascade of patterned reactions. We become filled with self-doubt and self-criticism. We call ourselves stupid or worthless or any other number of negative judgments, or we make these criticisms of others. Or we just try to deny the situation that caused us distress, choosing to ignore what we know in our heart to be true.

Humans, as patterned beings, will do everything that we can to fit our experience into our pre-existing patterns, even if those patterns are unhealthy and harmful to us. Why do we constantly do the same kinds of things that harm us, even when we recognize the harm that they cause? For example, when our spouse or partner says or does something that upsets us, instead of seeking to understand why we are upset—analyzing the pattern of action, reaction, and emotional state—we get upset and angry and then react in such a way that we *know* will only escalate the situation. Later, we probably apologize and might feel guilty and self-critical of our reaction. We justify it by saying "I'm only human," and ask for forgiveness.

The trouble is that most likely we're not forgiving ourselves for our actions, nor are we learning from the situation. This sets in place another pattern of ongoing self-judgment and criticism. This, then, becomes a negative emotional pattern and we then carry that emotional wound around with us everyday in our hearts and those emotions will affect other patterns. We might go to work and let our emotional negativity out on others in an attempt to make ourselves feel better. But our heart knows what we're doing, and while we may have the illusion that it makes us feel better, it doesn't. We've just given more power to the negative emotional, behavioral, and conceptual patterns that started this in the first place.

Breaking the Habit

WHAT A MESS! How do we get out? Patterns seem to be on automatic pilot and even when we want to break the patterns, it is extremely difficult to do so. People spend years in therapy to trying to alter their patterns. Some succeed. Some don't. It is terribly difficult to change a pattern when we are caught up in it, and most of the time we are not even aware that we are in a pattern. When we are aware, we tend to be judgmental of ourselves, which may make us feel like we're doing our required penance, but that does not put positive energy into changing the pattern. It only puts energy into punishing ourselves, which is itself a pattern of reaction, thought, and feeling.

We carry around these patterns with us all the time, and the patterns create emotional resonances that we carry in our hearts.

So we carry around these patterns with us all the time, and the patterns create emotional resonances that we carry in our hearts. Living with pain is difficult. We manage by creating more illusions to cover over the pain that we don't want to face and deal with. We create masks for ourselves so that we can project a certain pattern of ourselves into the world, but the mask won't make the pain go away. It only masks it.

Our masks help us to make our way in the world and help us to carry the burden of the emotional pain in our hearts, but they do not remove the pain. At best, they help us become numb so that we don't feel the pain, but the pain is still there. An emotional resonance doesn't just go away because we choose to ignore it or pretend that it is something other than what it is. The emotional resonance created by our patterns will be with us in our hearts until we deal with it. We carry our hearts with us in all places and in all times. If spiritual seekers want to clean out their hearts and lighten their burdens, they will need to understand their own patterns and how they resonate in their hearts.

Chapter 7, Main Points:

* Everything that exists is made of patterns.

* Every moment of existence is a further expression of countless, innumerable, intertwined and interconnecting patterns and systems of manifestation.

* Mushrooms can help spiritual seekers to perceive, understand, and make peace with the patterns that govern one's own particular manifestation in the world.

* Humans, as patterned beings, will do everything that we can to fit our experience into our pre-existing patterns, even if those patterns are unhealthy and harmful to us.

* The emotional resonance created by our patterns will be with us in our hearts until we deal with it.

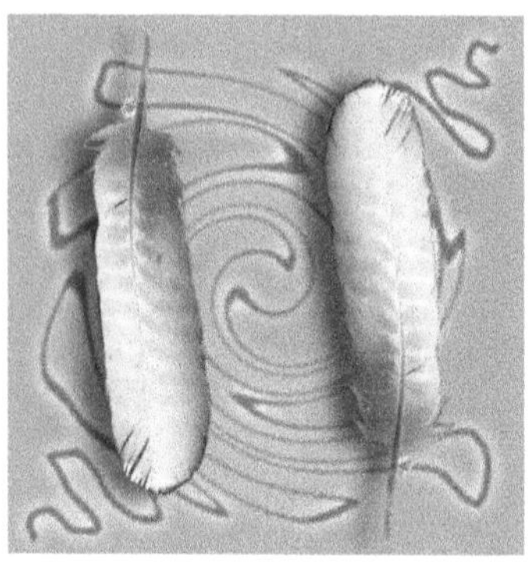

CHAPTER 8

Seeing the Patterns

Mushrooms show spiritual seekers the patterns of their being. Whether you want to take that statement as a metaphor or literal truth is a personal choice, and probably matters very little in the end, for the important thing is the experience and what one does with this understanding, not what is "real" or "imaginary."

Earlier I said that mushrooms show spiritual seekers themselves, which I described as looking into a spiritual mirror. If a person is a collection of patterns, then this is primarily what mushrooms are able to show seekers, at a very basic level. What seekers see in the spiritual mirror is their personal patterns and how they create emotional resonances in their heart. Learning to work with mushrooms is

> . . . then the patterns grew into architectural structures, with colonnades and architraves, patios of regal splendor, the stone-work all in brilliant colors
>
> -- Gordon Wasson

learning how to work with these patterns and ultimately change them, if need be. Mushrooms show and reveal much more than this, but for the purposes of the discussion here, this is the foundation of the kind of spiritual work under investigation.

> While tripping, I felt how I was embedded in the social and biological processes that were spun like the intricate filaments of a spider's web all around me. The world returned to the status of an original mystery, but nothing was more bizarre than my own consciousness, my place in the structure of all I could see and sense and know.
>
> -- Daniel Pinchbeck

Patterns, Patterns, Everywhere

MY UNDERSTANDING OF SPIRITUALITY and how mushrooms can contribute to spiritual awareness changed radically one day when a friend and I each ate 3.2 grams of dried psilocybin mushrooms. Early on in the experience, my attention was drawn to my friend. When I looked at him, I felt that I could actually see the patterns of his life. When one consumes psilocybin mushrooms, if they are strong enough, one will see flowing and undulating geometric patterns of amazingly intricate architecture everywhere, including in "empty" space. As I looked at my friend, I saw these geometric forms, but what I understood at the time was that these were *his* patterns. In those patterns, I saw that my friend, like everyone else, carried deep unresolved emotions within him that caused him to negatively judge himself. In short, my impression was that there were issues that my friend would benefit from addressing and changing.

I knew at the time that the mushrooms could show me how to help my friend, though I didn't understand how. I knew that it would require a great deal of work and that it would dredge up difficult issues that my friend would have to face.

I kept silent, however, and did not share any of this with my friend. Emotional pain and self-judgments that we make of ourselves are very difficult to face and I did not know how to get into this with my friend at that moment, though I do believe that if we had started working, the mushrooms would have shown the way.

I didn't know this then, but I fully believe it to be true now. If our heart knows the truth about ourselves, and the mushrooms show us ourselves, they will show us what we need to see and present to us that which we must face. If one is open to it, they will *always* do this. They are there, ready to teach and show the spiritual seeker, but one has to be open.

Instead of directing my attention to my friend, however, I turned my attention to myself. It was then that I began a profound nine-hour tutelage with the mushrooms that completely altered my understanding of my life and the world I construct about myself. I spent the journey looking into my heart and immersed myself in what the mushrooms had to teach me. What I found was that my own patterns were everywhere, in everything that I saw and experienced. I learned how to "get inside" these patterns but still maintain The Witness. There were extremely intense and difficult moments, and moments of profound and life-changing realizations.

In the end, I came out the other side with a sense of lightness and healing that had me walking on air for the next two weeks. I was filled with a joyous energy and Spirit was flowing through openly. I had looked into my heart, gone into my patterns, faced my fears and emotional pain and judgments and was released from them. Not all of them, of course, but those things that I most needed to deal with and address at that time of my life. I knew then that at any time in my life I could go back to the mushrooms to learn. Unresolved issues will resurface, and new issues will come to the surface as well. I thought of it as spiritual maintenance, a bit of a cosmic tune up.

Like a kind of spiritual maintenance unresolved and new issues surface—a bit of a cosmic tune up.

And through this, I had found a true sense of spiritual connection and awareness that I had never before achieved in my life. What had been abstract notions of spirituality, journeying, alchemical transformation, shamanic insight, and mystical rapture became something immediate and present in my being and my life.

Becoming Aware

THERE ARE MANY WAYS for spiritual seekers to recognize patterns, and while there may be some techniques that personally work for one person, they may or may not work for another. All spiritual seekers will need to explore their own patterns and find the most effective ways for them to identify and work with them. Once they do so, however, spiritual seekers can change themselves and their lives, and when done with conscious intent and awareness, the results can be profound and empowering.

Patterns are manifestations that carry information with them, and therefore any given pattern will carry some degree of information about any other pattern.

How does one begin to recognize and work with patterns? There are so many ways to do this. We are made of very rich and complex patterns, and all patterns are connected to others. As has been stated several times, patterns are embedded within patterns within patterns within patterns within patterns. One pattern will easily lead to another and the more one explores them the more the spiritual seeker will understand their intimate interconnectivity. At heart, all the patterns of the universe are connected together.

Patterns are manifestations that carry information with them, and therefore any given pattern will carry some degree of information about any other pattern. Nothing is completely isolated or cut off from everything else. Everything is connected and everything carries information, or put otherwise, has meaning.

Everything Means Something

This is perhaps the first lesson of working with mushrooms and patterns. *Everything* has meaning. Human minds are the creators of meaning, but we are also the creators of our own particular experience of the world, and therefore everything in our world has meaning for us in some way or capacity. There is *nothing* in our experience that is irrelevant or meaningless. Just like the contents of a dream where *we* create everything that happens and exists because it has some meaning for

If spiritual seekers get overwhelmed when they see and recognize these patterns, they should just go with it.

us, our construction of reality also has meaning for us in some way or another.

The meaning of a thing is the information that it carries for our experience of creating our world. We create our world and we create the meaning that the things in our world carry for us. Therefore *anything* in our experience has the potential to teach us about ourselves and our world.

Some things are far more powerful and carry much greater resonance for this kind of investigation, but it is a fundamental truth that *anything* seekers encounter or experience with mushrooms has relevance for understanding the self and how they create their world and manifest their patterns.

When the spiritual seeker truly experiences this revelation of meaning under the influence of mushrooms, it can be quite an overwhelming moment. Remember that we spend a great deal of time, effort, and energy creating illusions and masks for ourselves. Thus, much of who and what we are we hide or cover over in some way. We think that we can keep these things private, and hopefully even out of our daily consciousness, but when the mushrooms have opened the spiritual seeker up, there is *no place* for us to hide. All those things that we wanted to keep secret and all those mysteries of our self are staring back at us wherever we look, either without or within. Everything is a reflection of our own mind and the meaning of things are right there in front of us, whether we want them to be there or not.

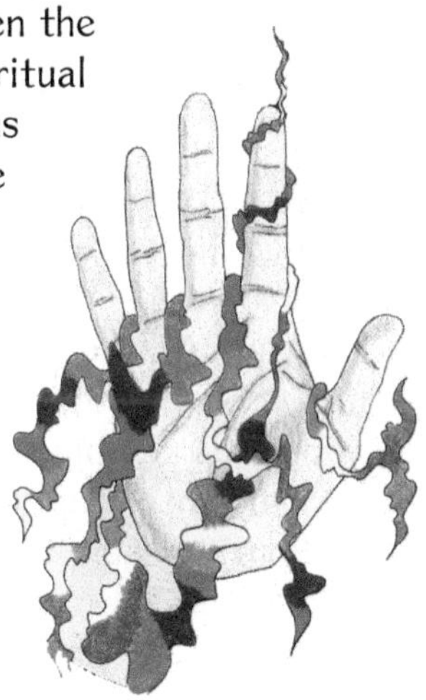

If spiritual seekers get overwhelmed when they see and recognize these patterns, they should just go with it. They shouldn't fight against it or try to stop it. They should accept it for what it is and then strive to work with it and explore it. Once they learn to work with the meanings of their patterns, they can begin to isolate particular aspects of them. They can take a complex subject and get into the part of the pattern that is most easily accessible to them at that time. All patterns are complex and spiritual seekers can explore multiple levels of them and their interconnections to other patterns. Spiritual seekers have to learn how to exert their power of choice, for they are the ones who ultimately choose what to dwell on within the revelation.

Inter-Connectivity and Layers of Meaning

IN QUANTUM PHYSICS, a fundamental concept is that of the quanta and the notion of a "quantum jump," also called a "quantum leap." Quanta are discrete collections of energy patterns. Sub-atomic particles, or "quarks," as a certain category of sub-atomic objects are called, seem to manifest their patterns at definite levels of energy. What this means is that when energy is put into a quantum system, we will not observe any change in the system until a critical amount of energy is introduced. When a critical point is reached, the quantum will "leap" to the next highest level of manifestation, or pattern of energy. Spatially, this might appear as an object suddenly disappearing in one "orbit" and then reappearing in another, instantaneously, without crossing the intervening space between the two "orbits."

The patterns that comprise a person's sense of being are somewhat similar to this process, though there is no need for an argument for any necessary correspondence between the two. But when they look at and analyze patterns, spiritual seekers find that there are somewhat distinct levels or layers to the patterns, some of which connect up with other patterns in ways that patterns at one level do not seem to do. They're all interconnected, but relatively speaking, they do seem to have particular layers of experience and emotional resonance that seekers can work through.

Similarly, we can also look at the physical world as relatively distinct patterns of manifestation starting from superstrings and working up through quarks, atomic particles, atoms, molecules, chemicals, material substances, macro-sized objects, and beyond. These levels are all interconnected. They are deeper and more surface ways of looking at and analyzing the patterns of manifestation in space-time.

The experience of our own patterns is very similar. There are layers. Some are more superficial and some are deeper. The deepest layers reside in our hearts. This is where the journey needs to take the spiritual seeker eventually, but one may need to work through many more surface layers before getting there. Once one has worked through them and cleaned out one's heart, Spirit can flow through unimpeded.

Observe; Don't Judge

For spiritual seekers to see their own patterns and work with them productively while experiencing mushrooms, they have to pay attention, be open, and must not judge themselves or what they perceive,

> The Witness is there to observe, experience, and learn. The Witness is not there to judge. If it were, it would be called "The Judge."

Judging yourself is not the same as being honest with yourself.

think, or feel. This is the action of The Witness. The Witness is there to observe, experience, and learn. The Witness is *not* there to judge. If it were, it would be called "The Judge." *The spiritual seekers who judge themselves will only become entrapped deeper in their own patterns and illusions.* That is what we do all the time. It doesn't help us and doesn't make us feel any better, so we are well-advised to avoid making such judgments. Easier said than done, but once one achieves The Witness, the difference between judging and looking honestly becomes immediately obvious. There is a vast difference here and worth exploring in greater detail.

Judging yourself is *not* the same as *being honest with yourself.* When we judge, we are working with our attachments of right and wrong, correct and incorrect. These are concepts that we create that do not necessary have any basis in reality. Most of our views of right and wrong are cultural, religious, and traditional creations that help us to function in society, but they are only concepts, some being more useful than others. They are not *necessary truths.* Clearly, ideas of right and wrong, moral and immoral change with every culture and every age. There is great relativity when it comes to human concepts of proper behavior and it is rare to find a proposition that all people in all cultures and all time agrees with universally.

Yet, these are the conceptual systems that we use to judge ourselves and others. This is not to say that morality and ethics are irrelevant, for we need such structures to function as societies with some basic rules of behavior and human interaction, but when we judge ourselves with somewhat arbitrary rules, we are not necessary recognizing reality, but rather our constructions of reality. Therefore being honest with yourself is not about judging. It is about looking dispassionately at what you find so that you can learn from what you see, and if necessary, choose to change your pattern. You may take morality and ethics into consideration when making such assessments, but ultimately, the goal is not to judge what you see and experience. Rather, the goal is to learn, transform, and empower.

Spiritual seekers should not judge what they see when they look at their patterns. This is difficult, as we have deep emotional resonances that well up when we do this work, but it is important for spiritual seekers to not get caught in the emotion. Seekers should let the emotion play out fully in all its depth and complexity so that it can be observed, but they should know that the emotion is their reaction and the result of their patterns of manifesting and creating their reality. They should not judge their emotion. They should let it be and strive to understand it.

Seeing patterns is all about striving to understand them—where they come from, how they manifest, what they mean for us, how they create different forms of emotional resonance in our hearts, and ultimately, how they impeded or assist in the free flowing of Spirit. This is *not* a passive process, though there certainly can be passive moments. Primarily, it is an active and introspective investigation into

Everything is a potential teacher.

our being and our process of manifesting reality. It requires careful thought and analysis.

> It is a fine balance between exerting control and letting the experience take one where it will.

Many people who take mushrooms enjoy the experience because they lose themselves in it. In a "good" trip this can be extremely pleasurable, profound even. But it is not using the experience to learn. It is done for enjoyment, entertainment, and perhaps a sense of spirituality, but not in the methodical sense that is under discussion here.

The Student

Looking at patterns with spiritual intent is about the spiritual seeker's willingness and desire to learn from them. To really see them for what they are, seekers need to think. They should invite the components of their mushroom experience to teach them. It is a learning experience. To learn, they have to be open to the tutelage. Anything and everything in the spiritual seekers' mushroom experience can teach them about themselves. Everything spiritual seekers experience is already embedded within their own patterns of reality manifestation. Everything they experience carries meaning and information. Everything is a potential teacher.

> The Witness allows spiritual seekers to step back and look that their patterns from a somewhat removed perspective.

In my initiatory experience with mushrooms, after I turned my attention to my own patterns of manifestation, I saw that the mushrooms could teach me and I invited them to do so. As soon as I did, I found that everything in my experience could impart wisdom and understanding. The deeper I went into the mushrooms, the easier it

was to see and understand that I could choose which aspects of my experience I wanted to include in my spiritual lessons. Just like waking into a dream, I had the power to change anything in my experience, at least in terms of how I chose to relate to things and let them express their meanings to me. I knew I could change what I allowed into my experience and what I wanted to work with. There was a profound sense of freedom in this realization. I had the power to navigate my inner world at will, yet also to surrender to it, freely accepting the lessons that came.

The spiritual seeker doesn't want to exert too much control, for then there is the risk of cutting one's self off from deeper potentials of the experience. It is a fine balance between exerting control and letting the experience take one where it will. The best advice is to trust in the mushrooms. They will show spiritual seekers the patterns that they need to see and give them the information that they need, when they need it. Trying to exert too much control can cut spiritual seekers off from these mushroom revelations. Too little control and they can spiral into an introspective hell where they lose sight of The Witness and instead see through the eyes of The Judge.

Looking through the eyes of the Judge is looking through the wounded heart as a wounded being. The Witness looks *into* the heart to clean it out. The Judge looks *through* the wounds in the heart and colors everything it sees with those wounds.

Fractals abound in nature, and when we have a passing understanding of them, they are easy to see and identify in all kinds of natural settings.

Collapsing Time

ONE WAY OF THINKING of working with patterns is the idea of "collapsing time." The fundamental nature of patterns is that they are processes of manifestation that persist and express themselves through time. Most of the time we are too caught up in the patterns to see their shape, their origins, and their paths that lead into the future. We often *feel* these patterns, and at least intuitively understand how they affect our emotional core. But when we are caught up in them, it is very difficult to see the way out, or to think of how we might act, think, feel, or be differently. The Witness, however, allows the spiritual seeker to take a step back and look at his patterns from a somewhat removed perspective.

We could compare The Witness to an out-of-body experience, except that it isn't necessarily quite so literal—though it can be. Spiritual seekers can find a place inside their mind and spiritual being that is outside of the main stream of their manifesting patterns. From that safe vantage, they can see where the river comes from, its course, and where it is going and the consequences that it will bring with it, and those that it has already caused.

In a sense, this is like "collapsing time." The spiritual seeker sees the pattern as a *process of manifestation that expresses itself through development in time*. Though spiritual seekers are still experiencing their manifesting patterns, The Witness stands just off to the side. This is where spiritual seekers want to put their attention. They should keep it with The Witness and they'll find that their perspective can span time in a way that is extremely difficult to achieve in otherwise normal circumstances.

Natural Fractals

IN A WAY patterns are similar to fractals. While there are different, specific kinds of fractals, such as the Mandelbrot set and the Julia set, these distinctions are not particularly relevant to our discussion. What is significant is that fractals are complex patterns that have been used to mathematically describe and map out patterns of change and development of objects in the physical world such as landforms, galaxies, and plant and animal anatomy and physiological development. What makes fractals so fascinating is that not only are they aesthetically beautiful and endlessly interesting to look at, but that they are also infinite. No matter what level we look at a fractal, we see the same patterns manifesting again and again and again. In other words, the large-scale pattern of a fractal is actually made of much smaller repetitions of the exact same pattern. Take any smaller part of the fractal, and you will find that it too is made of even smaller repetitions of the exact same pattern. The pattern goes all the way "up" and all the way "down."

The next time you are by a natural place with running water, do a little investigating. Take a river, for example. Look at the large-scale structure of the river and you see a particular course of the river that is shaped by the force of the river and the land that it flows through. Now look closer. Look at the patterns along the water bank. If conditions are right, you'll notice repetitions of similar patterns. Now look

even closer. Look at the rivulets in the sand where water has washed into the river. Look familiar? Now look even closer. Look at the miniature rivulets that feed into the main rivulets. See the pattern yet?

Of course what you see will not be as clean as a computer-generated fractal, but if conditions are good, you will see a striking amount of continuity in the patterns. Fractals abound in nature, and once we have a passing understanding of them, they are easy to see and identify in all kinds of natural settings from mountain ranges, shorelines, and cloud formations, to fern leaves, tree branches, or seashells.

Just like looking at one's patterns of manifestation as being similar to the levels of description in physics, so too can spiritual seekers look at their patterns as being similar to fractals. In fact, this is quite easy to do given that when one looks through eyes influenced by mushrooms, the mushroom eater will see patterns everywhere. When spiritual seekers think of them as *their* patterns, and as having direct meaning and information for them, they can start to work with them.

Just like the river, spiritual seekers have larger patterns that are made of smaller patterns, and they are made of even smaller patterns. Spiritual seekers can start anywhere they like, or wherever the mushrooms direct them to begin. When they get to the heart, they'll know it. To get there, they'll have to direct their attention.

Chapter 8, Main Points:

* Mushrooms will show the spiritual seeker the patterns of one's being.

* What one sees in the spiritual mirror are one's patterns and how they create emotional resonances in the heart. Learning to work with mushrooms is learning how to work with these patterns and ultimately change them, if need be.

* At heart, all the patterns of the universe are connected together. Patterns are manifestations that carry information with them, and therefore any given pattern will carry some degree of information about any other pattern. Nothing is completely isolated or cut off from everything else. Everything is connected and everything carries information and has meaning.

* To see one's own patterns, spiritual seekers have to pay attention, be open, and refrain from judging what they perceive, think, or feel. This is the action of The Witness. Judging one's self will only entrap the spiritual seeker deeper in his or her own patterns and illusions.

* Judging yourself is not the same as being honest with yourself.

* Seeing patterns is all about striving to understand them—where they come from, how they manifest, what they mean for us, and how they create different forms of emotional resonance in our heart, and ultimately, how they impeded or assist in the free flowing of Spirit.

CHAPTER 9

Directing Attention

SOMETHING QUITE WONDERFUL and extraordinary about mushrooms is that spiritual seekers can choose how to direct their attention and create their experience. Of course, this is *always* true, but most of the time we are too caught up in our patterns to exert this amount of control consciously. Ideally, learning to work with mushrooms should teach one how to begin to exert this kind of control in everyday life, for in reality, the entheogen experience is no different from one's normal experience. Mushroom eaters are just oriented to their experience of reality-manifestation in a new and unique way.

> . . . I was basically in charge of what I could perceive and think about, that I was not bound by external forces but rather made choices that determined the extent and quality of my awareness.
>
> -- Ralph Metzner

The basic process of reality-manifestation and creation continues on as it did before and will continue to do so after. In this sense, there is nothing that one can do, accomplish, or experience while working with mushrooms that one can't in ordinary consciousness, though the level of intensity and profundity of meaning will be of a very different degree. However, it is important to recognize that in many respects, this kind of work is fundamentally richer and more easily accessed and understood while enraptured in the entheogen experience. It is a strange paradox, for the experience is so fundamentally different, yet completely intimate and familiar, the closest and farthest thing at the same time.

> But if I concentrated on the vision, the hut receded. I had control of my will and intellect. I was able to point my mind in any direction, though I felt I was in turn influenced by the emotional content of the visions, much as emotions influence the mind in normal circumstances.
>
> -- Frederick Swain

The Pull of Emotions

WHAT WE FIND IN OUR ORDINARY CONSCIOUSNESS is that it is extremely difficult to deal with challenging emotions and judgments because the emotional resonance has such a strong hold over us. Once we give our attention to these things, we can easily get caught by them and become trapped in the drama we've created for ourselves. We talk about being "in a slump" or "spiraling into depression," or "losing control." These are all signs of having our attention caught by a negative resonance.

This is why we invest so much energy and effort in avoiding, repressing, and masking over our pain and wounds. We don't want to face them because we feel that we will get caught by them. But often we can't keep up the energy of defending our illusions and our protections from our wounds and the pain takes hold and we sink into depression, judgment, and brutal self-criticism. We then seek relief by transferring our negative emotions to others or into our relationships, or we hurt others to make ourselves feel better. It's a vicious cycle, only making us feel better temporarily, at best, and our heart records our emotional and judgmental transgressions, waiting to suck us back in later. Though not healthy, this is a pattern of manifestation that virtually everyone falls into at times, and some are completely consumed by such cycles of pain and suffering.

Entheogens allow spiritual seekers the opportunity to reorient how they align their attention and their sense of identity

The problem is that we give over our attention to these cycles and judgments and let ourselves get caught in their illusions and pain. We identify with the cycle rather than perceiving it as what it is—a pattern of manifestation that we can choose to let carry us away or not. We think that we *are* that, when all that is really happening is that we've chosen to let our attention reside there and we identify with it.

Spiritual Reorientation

ENTHEOGENS ALLOW SPIRITUAL SEEKERS the opportunity to reorient how they align their attention and their sense of identity. When one experiences mushrooms, it becomes obvious that where one chooses to give his or her attention is what determines the seeker's experience of manifesting reality. Do they choose to put their attention into wallowing in self-pity, judgment, and blame, or do they choose to let their attention perceive the conditions, thoughts, and patterns that give rise to these negativities and observe the consequences that will result?

Nothing is ever just one thing.

Managing one's attention is crucial for working with mushrooms. Some aspects of spiritual seekers' introspection in the spiritual mirror will be much more difficult than others. They can help navigate the difficulty by managing their attention. If seekers feel that they are in danger of getting caught in the emotional resonance rather than observing and contemplating it, they can change their attention by bring something else into their experience. They can consider a different aspect of the pattern. They can examine a different level. They can find another emotional resonance that is connected with the pattern that is easier for them to deal with at that time. They have the power to change their experience and they should use this power.

Many Ways of Looking

NOTHING IS EVER JUST ONE THING. All patterns are complex and interconnected with other patterns, some of which are more dominant and influential, others less so. Emotions are complex as well. We rarely feel *only one way* about things in our lives.There are always multiple aspects to our emotions, our reactions, our behaviors, and our judgments. At times certain patterns may seem so overwhelming that we might convince ourselves that it can only be as we are experiencing it at that time, but this is rarely, if ever, the case. There's always another way to look at and contemplate our emotions and the experiences of our lives.

In this sense, a hellish trip on mushrooms can almost instantaneously transform into a beatific experience when the person chooses to shift attention to something else within the experience. If seekers feel that they've gone as far as they can with a particular issue at a given time, then they should give their attention to something else. Conscious spiritual seekers are masters of the mushroom experience. They make the choice.

We might not be able to control situations, but we can always be the masters of our responses and how we choose to look at our experiences.

Often we don't realize that this is a choice and we feel victimized by our emotions and judgments, or situations that appear to be completely outside of our influence or control, but this is not the necessary state of being. We choose. Our reactions to thoughts, emotions, or situations, no matter how difficult or disturbing, are always a matter of choice. We might not be able to control situations, but we can always be the masters of our responses and how we choose to look at our experiences.

Choices with Integrity

TO CHOOSE RESPONSES WISELY, we must be willing to look at the things we don't want to see and consider them in their fullness and their depth. What we don't want to do, but do most of the time, is merely transfer attention from one set of illusions to another, or take off one mask and put on another, so to speak. Spiritual seekers want to understand their emotions, understand the consequences of personal choices, and then, with full conscious awareness and intent, choose the path or pattern that will free them from making judgments of their choices and actions. This is how spiritual seekers keep their hearts clean. They make conscious choices generated from their sense of self-honesty and integrity.

> If there is a "hell," it is certainly made of the unresolved judgments we make of ourselves.

When we put our attention into choices that *we know in our hearts do not come from honesty and integrity, we deposit negative emotional resonances in our hearts that we will have to deal with sooner or later.* Isn't it far better to deal with it now and empower ourselves than to put it off or pretend that it isn't there?

Spiritual seekers may ask themselves: What do I want there to be in my heart when I die? Do I want a clean heart that allows Spirit to flow through freely and lets the pure light of being shine through, or do I want a heart encrusted with wounds that will cause me to judge myself and encloses me in darkness?

Master of Attention

TO WORK WITH ENTHEOGENS PRODUCTIVELY and consciously, spiritual seekers must manage their attention. They can use their attention as a tool of their spirit. They use it as a diamond to cut through all illusions. They use it to explore their self, their heart, and their being. They direct it, or let themselves be directed by the mushrooms, to that which they must see. Their attention is their greatest tool. They don't squander it.

> While experiencing mushrooms, one can easily get distracted or off course. In mushrooms consciousness, what might have been a fleeting thought or momentary daydream in ordinary consciousness can take on epic proportions .

To really use one's attention, the spiritual seeker has to *pay attention.* If spiritual seekers approache the mushroom experience with the mindset of "What can I learn from this?" and "What can you teach me?" then they've taken the first step. We might call this *setting intention.* However, setting one's intention is largely meaningless unless one has also committed to actively and consciously using one's attention to navigate the mushroom experience.

Spiritual seekers choose what they give their attention to. While the possibilities for spiritual experience and revelation are rich when using mushrooms, seekers should turn their attention to understanding their patterns, how they manifest and create their reality. Just like in ordinary consciousness, while experiencing mushrooms, one can easily get distracted or get off course. What might have been a fleeting thought or momentary daydream in ordinary consciousness can take on epic proportions while experiencing mushrooms. Conscious spiritual seekers will think about what they are doing and experiencing, measuring their emotions, their reactions, their thoughts. They ask themselves, "Am I getting lost in mushroom absorption, or am I actually using the mushrooms?"

Spiritual seekers strive to make the most of the mushroom experience, taking great pains not to waste the precious fleeting moments of revelation and spiritual wonder. Spiritual seekers repeatedly ask themselves whether they are giving their attention to something that is really going to teach them something, or are they just getting lost watching the grass grow? This is not to say that watching the grass—or the carpet!—grow can't be a pleasant and novel experience, for surely it can. But why is the spiritual seeker taking mushrooms? What is the intention and how are they using their attention to achieve their intention?

Using entheogens isn't a vacation or just time to play in the psychedelic playground.

Spiritual seekers eat mushrooms to engage in spiritual work. Using entheogens isn't a vacation or just time to play in the psychedelic playground. It's spiritual work that requires vigilance and concentration. Lessons given by mushrooms and the revelations they bring can be fleeting, their possibility of empowerment fading quickly. It is both one's intention and one's attention that can make the difference in really integrating these lessons into daily life.

When spiritual seekers are really using their attention, they can see the patterns of their lives. They provide us with courses of action, thought, and emotional reaction. To some extent, we need these patterns to make our way in the world and there is certainly nothing fundamentally wrong with them. The problem is that often our patterns entrap us in negative cycles that generate negative emotional resonances and self-judgments. The goal of using our attention to identify our patterns is not so that we can rid ourselves of the patterns. Rather, it is to give us the chance to look at them honestly and determine what we can do to alter the patterns or influence them more positively through our choices.

We all have natural tendencies to be particular ways. We call this our personality and our natural talents and abilities. There are some things that are very difficult to change, and others that are easier. If we want to change a pattern, we need to consider it carefully. If we find that we are inclined to behave or react in a particular way, we can use our attention to explore the roots of that pattern and what affect it has on us, our experience, and on others. Spiritual seekers use their attention to assess what this pattern means

to them from a position of total honesty and integrity. If it is something that they can change or alter, they consider how. They let the new pattern play out in their mind and test the consequences. They adjust it, if necessary. Their attention is their tool. They use it to explore the profound vistas of meaning and possibility that mushrooms will open up to them.

Accepting Limits of Change

THERE WILL ALWAYS BE SOME THINGS about one's self that spiritual seekers cannot change, but by using their attention, they can alter how these things that they cannot change create emotional resonance in their heart. In this sense, spiritual seekers look to their reactions to those things that remain outside of their direct control. They accept the limits of what they can change, and then investigate what they can alter in their reactions.

When confronted by something negative that spiritual seekers cannot change, for example, do they beat themselves up because of it? Do they create themselves in the image of a victim? Do they transpose their negative emotions onto others in frustration and self-judgment? Using their attention, spiritual seekers find that there may be something they cannot change, but they can change the way they let this affect them and their experience of themselves and their world. Is it something that they just need to accept and stop repressing, denying, or masking over?

> I saw how my quest for spiritual consciousness led me to the experience and how the questions I long sought answers to were coming to fruition right before me.

These are often precisely the patterns that spiritual seekers see in the mushroom experience because these are the things that cause us the most emotional pain and

I learned how to look at myself and the world in an entirely new way.

suffering and are the aspects of our being that most need addressing. These are the hardest patterns to face because of the urge to try and escape them. Conscious seekers know, however, that if they can't change one aspect of the pattern, they can look more closely and they'll probably find at least some part that they can change.

This is the beauty of working with mushrooms. Our patterns set out the conditions for what we are probable to do, think, and feel, but our patterns do not fully determine us. While we are predisposed to act and react in certain manners, we can always exert our will and effort to alter the course of the pattern, if only slightly. The mushrooms help one to see what can be changed as well as help one make peace with what cannot be changed. If one does this correctly, it *will* clean the heart. It takes careful attention, effort, and a willingness to face the darkness, but it can be done.

A Life Review

IN MY MUSHROOM INITIATION, my experience of these issues was set within the context of a life review. At the time I thought that my experience was similar to the phenomenon of one's life "flashing before one's eyes" just before the moment of death. I saw all the patterns of my life from childhood up to the present and then extending on into the future. I saw how my beliefs, thoughts, judgments, and emotional reactions had worked to shape me and bring me to that point in the present moment. I was able to see how my quest for spiritual consciousness had led me to the experience and how

the questions I long sought answers to were coming to fruition right before me. I saw what I could change and knew what I could not change. I looked into my heart and learned how to be true to myself, how to be honest with myself, and how to treat myself with the integrity and respect I deserved as a human being.

I saw how my patterns and illusions affected others, as well as myself, and I saw how I treated others was simply a mirror for how I treated myself. I looked into my heart and I cleaned it out, and when I did, Spirit flowed openly and freely through me. I knew who I was, and in that moment, I found a faith that I had never had before in my life. I found a faith in the reality that we *are* more than our illusions of self. I found faith in the universe as a collective whole that is bound together by love and light and the never ceasing creative and expressive power of Spirit. I learned that the only true way of interacting with others is with compassion, integrity, and honesty, for we are all in this together, continually striving to increase the creative potential of the universe though our own self-awareness and our universal experience of life and death. We are the universe looking back at itself and I learned that my heart and the heart of the universe are one and the same.

It was a beautiful and profound experience for me, and it changed my life. I used my attention in a capacity that I never had before. My attention was brought back to the process of becoming, of how I manifested myself and my reality in the world and I learned how to look at myself and the world in an entirely new way. My eyes were open, and my attention became my tool to see what I had to see and know what I had to know. I gained a perspective on my life and sense of self and identity that had never been present before. I collapsed time and saw my past, present, and future, all in one inexpressible moment of the ever-present now, that intangible yet eternally existent matrix of continual becoming.

I felt myself to be the recipient of a profound grace, but also to be an active participant in my own spiritual adventure, for my intention had helped to set me on this path and helped to bring this experience to me. While it wasn't as I might have expected, I found what I had set out to find—a sense of spiritual meaning and purpose.

Chapter 9, Main Points:

* Mushrooms allow spiritual seekers the opportunity to reorient how they align their attention and our sense of identity.

* If spiritual seekers feel they've gone as far as they can with a particular issue at a given time, then they can give their attention to something else. The spiritual seeker is the master.

* When we put our attention into choices that we know in our hearts do not come from honesty and integrity we deposit negative emotional resonances in our hearts that we will have to deal with sooner or later.

* Attention is the spiritual seeker's greatest tool. To really use one's attention, one has to pay attention.

* The goal of using one's attention to identify patterns is not so that we can rid ourselves of the patterns. Rather, it is to give us the chance to look at them honestly and determine what we can do to alter the patterns.

* There will be some things about one's self that we cannot change, but by using one's attention, the spiritual seeker can alter how these things create emotional resonance in the heart.

CHAPTER 10

Setting Intention

MUSHROOMS SHOW SPIRITUAL SEEKERS what they need to see whether or not they are looking for them to do so. However, the intentions of the one consuming the mushrooms can make a profound difference.

When the mushrooms initiated me, I had come to the experience with many questions, thoughts, and intentions that were different from earlier experiences with mushrooms where I wanted to have psychedelic fun and experience something novel. Unlike those earlier experiences, this time I wanted to learn and I wanted to find that magic that I hoped was there but had no necessary faith in. I was looking to have such an experience and was fortunate, for it came to me.

They are psychedelic experiences. Their authenticity comes from themselves

Would it have happened if my intentions had been otherwise? In some sense yes, and in some sense no. Mushrooms show spiritual

> For those who seek the hidden depths of the unconscious mind, the possibilities of exploration are unlimited. The variations are endless. One can enter mythological realms and mental worlds undreamed of. If one gives spiritual meaning to these experiences, as the Indians do, the results are far more significant.
>
> -- Frederick Swain

seekers what they need to see, but if seekers aren't paying attention, or are letting themselves get distracted or caught up in the drama and novelty of the experience, they might not realize what is happening. This is what happened to me one night when I ate mushrooms and had a "bad trip," wandering around in a state of self-judgment and self-criticism. The mushrooms were showing me myself and my emotional reactions and judgments, but I was too caught up in the drama of the experience to realize that I could use it as a precious tool to honestly examine myself and my life. Instead, I sank into criticism and self-punishment. I felt stupid, foolish, embarrassed, and low. I could have turned the experience around, but I didn't know that I could and I didn't know how.

That time, my intention was to have "fun" with my college roommate and share in the strange and wonderful experience that is mushrooms, something I had newly been introduced to. Several years later, when my perspective on mushrooms was quite different, having spent some time studying shamanism and comparative mysticism academically, I came to the experience with an entirely different mindset. I did not come to the experience looking to have "fun." My *intention* was very different at that time, even if I didn't fully understand how this would change the experience. I was looking for something sacred, something empowering, something transformative and spiritually meaningful.

As They Are Treated, So They Will Be

ONE'S INTENTION CANNOT CONTROL or determine the experience that unfolds once the mushrooms set to work, just like we cannot determine or control the world around us. Many people have very clear intentions to grow spiritually but feel frustrated and blocked in their progress. Anthropological literature is full of accounts of people seeking visions and shamanic wisdom only to find themselves frustrated and disappointed that the spirits did not come to them and did not impart a gift of empowerment. Certainly many such people were sincere in their intentions and determination, but for whatever reason, it didn't happen for them. The lesson is that we cannot determine how Spirit will speak to us or what lessons it will impart or the gifts it will give. Spirit will make its own choices.

The most effective spiritual workers are those who strive to get out of the way and to be a conscious conduit for Spirit.

Even so, intention is a powerful tool and, in most instances, greatly increases spiritual seekers' chances of finding what they are seeking, though the response will often come in an unexpected and unusual form that is not at all determined by the seeker. However, for our intention to be truly effective, it must come from a well of honesty and integrity. Setting intention is not about seeking selfish fulfillment or setting desires on something for the purpose of ego attachment. In other words, spiritual seekers' intention are not necessarily about what *they* want as ego-centered beings. Really, the most effective intention is the intention to *get one's self out of the way so that Spirit may flow through freely and unimpeded.* It is our illusions and attachments to self and our selfish and our selfish desires that block the flow of Spirit. To truly set spiritual intention is to have the intention of dispersing illusions and seeing through the deceptions we create for ourselves. The most effective spiritual worker is the one who strives to get out of the way and be a conscious conduit for Spirit.

To put the matter another, and perhaps simpler, way, is to say that one's intention should be to approach mushrooms as being *sacred* and the experience as being something *sacred.* Spiritual seekers treat them as sacred. They honor the mushroom experience as being sacred. They honor mushrooms for the gift and blessing that they are.

Just as our interactions with others are mirrors of how we treat ourselves, so too is our treatment of mushrooms a mirror of how we treat ourselves.

Spiritual seekers always remember that the way they treat the mushrooms, and the mushroom experience, is the way they treat themselves. Just as our interactions with others are mirrors of how we treat ourselves, so to is our treatment of mushrooms. Those looking to use mushrooms to have fun and fulfill ego-centered desires is how they treat others, and how they treat themselves and their lives. Is that coming from a center of integrity and honesty, or is it something else? Genuine spiritual seekers aren't afraid to ask themselves the hard questions and take an honest look at the answer. Honesty is *the only way to have intention with integrity.*

Lying is not bad simply because it is "immoral" or somehow "wrong." Religions have countless proscriptions and restrictions and codes for behavior, thought and action. These are fine if they help us reach a point of honesty and integrity, but nothing is *necessarily* right or wrong. But different thoughts, behaviors, and actions do affect our connection to and experience of Spirit and the sacred. Lying, deception, and falsehoods are bad because they cut off our experience of Spirit and wrap us in our self-centered beliefs.

If we are honest with ourselves, then our intention is clear and we act with integrity. Spiritual seekers treat themselves with integrity and honesty, and they do the same with others—the mushrooms included. They treat mushrooms as sacred because they accept their own sacredness and the sacredness of their own experience. They welcome of the power of Spirit and the revelations of truth that follow. It is their intention to let these come to them without judgment or expectation, accepting all that they see and find, bringing every lesson home and welcoming it into their hearts.

Something is only sacred if we perceive it as such. That is the power of our intention.

Creating The Sacred Through Action

THE NOTION OF "THE SACRED" is an interesting concept. We can just as easily say "nothing is sacred" as we can say "everything is sacred." "Sacred" is a category of the human mind and we can choose to apply it to what we will. Nothing is intrinsically sacred. It is our thoughts, attitudes, behaviors, and beliefs about it that *create* the sacred. Therefore we can choose where to invest our notion of the sacred.

Something is only sacred *if we perceive it as such.* That is the power of our intention. If we intend to treat something as sacred, then it is sacred. It's that simple! If you think that mountain there is sacred and you set that intention from a well of integrity and honesty, then it's a sacred mountain. If you think that book on your shelf is sacred and you come to it from

Actions are intentions in motion.

an intention of honesty and integrity, then it's a sacred book. If one thinks that mushrooms are sacred, then they are sacred to that person.

But "the sacred" is not just about what we think or believe. Far more importantly, sacredness is how we act. Actions are our intentions in motion. "Actions speak louder than words," conventional wisdom proclaims, and it's true. We can say "this is sacred" all we want, but if our actions don't coincide with our words, then we are lying, or at least engaged in self-deception. When we honestly have the intention that something is sacred, we treat it as such. *That* is what makes something sacred—our clear intention and the actions that follow from it.

Spiritual Protection

WHEN SPIRITUAL SEEKERS SET THEIR INTENTION with honesty and integrity, they can act in the world with impunity in the sense that they have no need to judge or criticize themselves, even if they don't reach their goal. This is true for *all* of our actions and experiences, but it is crucial for the spiritual seeker's experience with mushrooms. If it is easy to beat ourselves up with self-criticism in ordinary consciousness, and we all know that it is, we can only imagine the power of this self-punishment when under the influence of mushrooms. Now *that* is some real suffering! Setting intention is a tool for not only influencing the shape of our experiences, but it is also a method of spiritual protection.

Everything one experiences with mushrooms is ultimately a reflection of one's self. If mushroom eaters experience themselves chased by demons, the demons are coming after them because some part of them thinks they deserve it.

Protection from what? From our self, of course! In some sense, everything one experiences with mushrooms is ultimately of one's self. If mushroom eaters experience themselves chased by demons, *they* are the source of those demons, and even if they can't admit it to themselves, the demons are coming after them because *some part of them thinks they deserve it*. If they set their intention with honesty and integrity, the demons have no real power, even if they are there. When spiritual seekers have honesty and integrity in their heart, they can bravely face the demons and learn from them. They know that what they are experiencing is sacred and they accept it as such.

Discovering the Sacred

HOW DOES ONE "TREAT" ENTHEOGENS AS SACRED? That, ultimately, is up to each and every spiritual seeker. No one can tell anyone else how to treat something as sacred or even what the sacred is. That is something that everyone will have to discover and explore for themselves.

If the rules of your religion help you set your intention from a place of honesty and integrity, then those are good rules because they bring you closer to the sacred.

Religions and spiritual traditions have all kinds of rules for treating something as sacred. Perhaps you know and live by some of these rules. If they help you set your intention from a place of honesty and integrity, then those are good rules in the sense that they serve the purpose of bringing you closer to the sacred. Often, however, the rules of religion regarding "the sacred" have nothing at all to do with setting one's intention from a position of honesty and integrity. Many of the rules and dogmas of religion are about control, fear, punishment, and judgment. Such views do far more harm than good. How many wars have been fought because people can't agree about what is "sacred" and what is "correct" or "incorrect" behavior towards the sacred? Human history is full of self-righteous violence and carnage, all in the name of the sacred.

The history of religions is largely one of vicious judgment, violence, and horrible offenses against humanity, the world, and yes, "the sacred." So if we come from a religious tradition, we should think about what helps us set our intention from a position of honesty and integrity so that we can approach and experience the sacred without judgment of ourselves or *anyone else.*

Followers of the world's religions are constantly judging each other, accusing each other of being false, sinful, evil, corrupt. We fill our hearts and minds with these lies and then we expend countless amounts of energy and effort killing and torturing each other to prove our point and live out our righteous delusions. It's time for humanity to grow up. We should jettison the superstitions, false beliefs, lies, and corruption.

Genuine spiritual experience has nothing to do with religion, though spiritual experience can be a part of religion. If our religion helps us reach the sacred, then we should be thankful and grateful. But we must look honestly. Does your religion fill you with fear, judgment, feelings of superiority or worthlessness? Does your religion promote hatred and

The spiritual seeker creates and discovers the sacred through ritual.

fear of others and intolerance? Does your religion constantly try and change people and force them to believe something that is not true for them and their own spirit? If so, then maybe it is more a hindrance than help in the experience of the sacred.

So when it comes to treating mushrooms as sacred, it does not mean that one needs to find some way to fit them into any pre-existing religion or mold, though spiritual seekers certainly can if they find that doing so helps them set their intention clearly and with honesty and integrity. What it does mean is that spiritual seekers should think carefully about how they treat mushrooms and their experience with them.

Spiritual seekers always ask themselves what they do to recognize that they are sacred and answer honestly. They question what they do to align their action with their intention. They make the experience sacred through their own sense of discovery, creativity, and sacred action.

Chapter 10, Main Points:

* Spiritual seekers cannot determine how Spirit will speak to them or what lessons it will impart or gifts it will give. One can, however, influence it with one's intentions.

* The most effective intention is the intention to get one's self out of the way so that Spirit may flow through freely and unimpeded.

* The spiritual seeker's intention should be to approach mushrooms as being sacred and the experience as being something sacred.

* One's actions are one's intentions in motion.

* No one can tell us how to treat something as sacred or even what the sacred is. That is something that all spiritual seekers have to discover and explore for themselves.

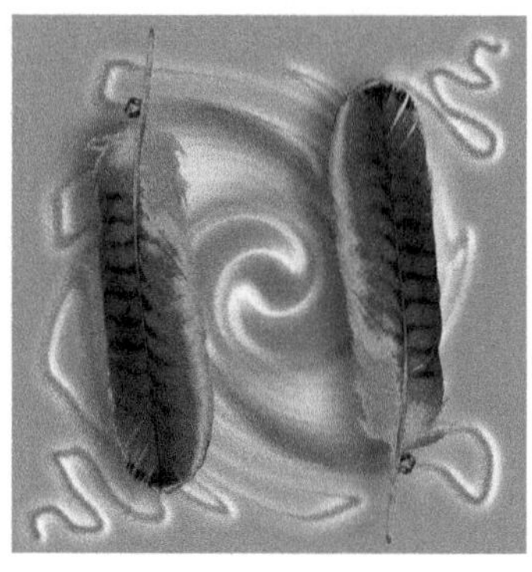

CHAPTER 11

The Art of Ritual

RITUALS CAN BE WONDERFUL AND POWERFUL. Virtually all traditional cultures that make use of visionary plants—and there are *many* such cultures—use these powerful plant allies in the context of rituals. There are communal rituals, such as the consumption of peyote in the Native American Church, initiatory rituals such as with the use of iboga in Africa, and countless shamanic healing rituals that have been used throughout the world and throughout history such as the shamanic mushroom rituals of Maria Sabina of the Mazatecs.

> When mushroom use is ritualized—guided by veteran users who can help orchestrate the necessary variables with careful attention to set and setting—an extraordinarily gratifying cerebral adventure can unfold.
>
> -- Paul Stamet

While there are incredibly diverse traditions, what they all have in common is that they use rituals to *set the intention* of the participants on the sacred nature of the activity and very importantly, to *provide a structure* for the experience. The ritual provides a structure for actions and induces a clear mindset. It provides a safety net of structure that allows participants to know and anticipate what is happening and what is coming next. Rituals allow one to begin, experience, and end different phases of the spiritual journey.

> Ritual can become a safeguard if the going gets rough—it can help lead you through the experience and make it profoundly meaningful. After repeated sessions, the ritual becomes a psychological road map, providing a framework for safe tripping. Rituals are built from the lessons learned from previous good experiences. But at some point, for the shamans among us, being safe is not the priority—pushing the envelope to new revelations is.
>
> -- Paul Stamet

Ritual Elements

THERE ARE SOME fairly universal elements of ritual that any ritual artist will want to take into consideration when creating a ritual or structures for ritual practice.

Rituals can be loosely constructed, organic, and spontaneous, or tightly structured and adhere to a strict form of action. What they still hold in common, however, is that at the very least there is often the transition between beginning, middle, and end. Keep in mind, however, that the "beginning" may be initiated long before any definitive "ritual" has taken place. A "ritual" per se often occurs at a set place at a set time, but getting there, preparing for it, and planning for it can also be an integral part of the ritual and should not be overlooked or ignored.

Rituals can be loosely constructed, organic, and spontaneous, or tightly structured and adhere to a strict form of action.

Something else that virtually all rituals incorporate is specific kinds of sensory stimuli. There is the use of sound, color, lighting, smells. This is especially important for entheogens rituals given their profound sensory nature. How things smell, how they look, and the lights and colors of an environment are crucially important and should be considered carefully for their effects and influences.

Space is also of great importance. All rituals take place somewhere—they don't just happen out in abstract space. Most rituals have various proscriptions for how the body should be used in the physical space, how symbols should be used, and how sound should be used. There are no universal rules here aside from the fact that ritual is seen as a unique time in a unique space. Any space can be made into a ritual space or a sacred space, but once it has been transformed, behaviors, thoughts, and attitudes tend to be transformed as well for the duration of the ritual and often beyond.

Lastly there are the symbols and ceremonial clothing used in rituals. Putting on different clothes, symbols, or jewelry for ritual greatly influences those participating. Even a small symbol, token, or piece of jewelry or object of power might be enough to alter someone's mindset. For more formal rituals, generally more attention is paid to these factors. They are always important, however, and ritual practitioners should find what changes in appearance, use of symbols, or clothing are appropriate for them.

One final word of advice: In general, I recommend that when conducting a mushroom ceremony that practitioners have everything they think they will want or need at the beginning of the ritual. Have the things needed or know where they are. The spiritual practitioner should avoid being distracted by unnecessary tasks so having everything ready helps ensure a sense that everything is in its place and accessible when needed.

Creating Ritual

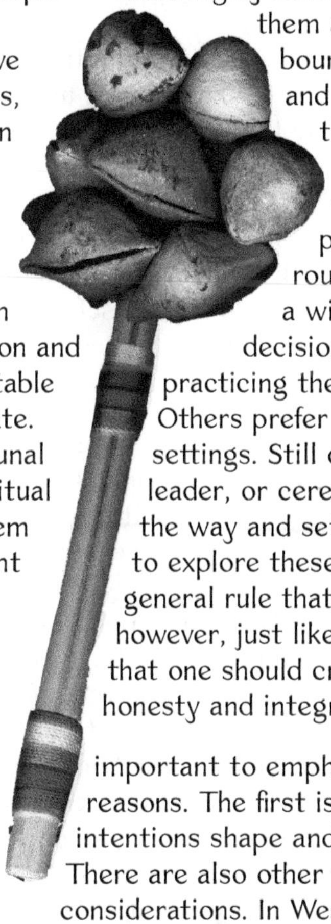

IT IS IMPOSSIBLE TO JUDGE beforehand who will respond to any particular form of ritual or spiritual practice. Some people need highly structured rituals, giving them a strong sense of protective boundaries, proscribed actions, and behavioral limits. Others gain the most benefit from a casually developed ritual, or a loose collection of practices, structures, and routines that provide them with a wide space for individual action and decision. Some are more comfortable practicing their rituals alone and in private. Others prefer more public and communal settings. Still others want a clear shaman, ritual leader, or ceremonial guide to show them the way and set the stage. Others want to explore these things for themselves. A general rule that will apply to all situations, however, just like with anything else, is that one should create ritual from a place of honesty and integrity.

This is *very* important to emphasize, for a variety of reasons. The first is because of how our intentions shape and guide our experience. There are also other very important considerations. In Western culture, the practices associated with "spirituality," as opposed to the traditional practice of "religion," are commonly collectively known as New Age. A very common practice of New Age spirituality is to borrow elements, rituals, symbols, and concepts from various traditions such as Native American, Buddhist, Hindu, Kabbalah. What many New Agers don't necessarily recognize, or pay the proper respect to, is that adherents of these traditions can be critical about "borrowing," which they often see as stealing or misappropriating.

Spiritual Inspiration vs Appropriation

A WIDESPREAD VIEW among Native Americans, for example, is that their traditions and rituals have been plundered by those seeking spirituality outside the context of mainstream religious institutions. There are countless books proclaiming to tell the eager spiritual seeker how use Native American rituals for "personal power" and all kinds of other claims. While many may find these books useful, it is important to understand the emotional distress that they cause others.

Given the shamanic nature of many indigenous traditions, and the intrinsically shamanic nature of entheogen experiences, it might seem very natural to take Native American rituals, symbols, and practices and fit them to the context of mushroom rituals, for example. However, such a view often fails to recognize one of the most important facts of Native American religions. These traditions are religions of particular cultures and places. Native American religions and rituals are not necessarily meant to be taken outside of the context of the actual physical place in which they are practiced. Really, one could reasonably claim that Native traditions have very little translatable meaning outside of their original contexts, given how strongly they are wedded to people and place. This is not to say that there is nothing universal within Native Traditions, but it is to say that the cultural identity of Native traditions is definitive.

It is common, however, for non-Natives to want to perform a "Lakota" vision quest, or do a Sundance, or sweat lodge, for example. Being invited to participate in such rituals is a great honor, but some decide to try their hand at conducting these rituals outside of their indigenous contexts. Such practices are often deemed disrespectful and hurtful to Native Americans. While participants may feel greatly rewarded by such rituals, the danger is that such practices set up the conditions for later judgment, accusations, and emotional distress. It raises questions of honesty and integrity. Such is not conducive to conditions that will allow ritual participants feel a clean heart, free from judgment and criticism. The lure of the exotic and the spiritually "other" is strong, but it is a spiritual pitfall, and one that should be avoided, and at the very least, considered very carefully.

What's the point of borrowing from others' rituals? Wise spiritual seekers are advised to make their own rituals. Trust in yourself and your own authenticity. If a Native American or Buddhist or Taoist or anyone else teaches spiritual seekers how to do something or how to use a ritual and they feel that it is authentic and true, then they should by all means use it. But don't appropriate. Don't steal spirituality.

Trust in yourself and your own authenticity.

Have confidence in your innate capacity to connect to and create the sacred. Humans are ritual-creating beings. What are rituals but highly stylized *patterns of actions*? Rituals make use of our natural state of being as pattern-manifesting reality creators. Rituals structure it, give it meaning, and connect us with the sacred.

So when we create our own rituals, we should think carefully and honestly about what we choose to do or incorporate into our ritual art. This can't be stressed enough. If we choose poorly, then we're setting ourselves up for negative emotional resonance and self-judgment and outright negative experiences. Spiritual seekers want their motives and choices to be unimpeachable. The conscious spiritual seeker strives to create conditions that renders self-criticism unnecessary.

A Sense of Ritual

In my own use of mushrooms, many of the elements that I incorporate into my ritual practice have Native American origins. Though I am not Native, through my work as a graduate student, I had the fortunate opportunity to study with Native American medicine people —in particular, with Mescalero Apache medicine people. They gave me instruction on how to use various forms of ritual action and I was given various gifts, such as eagle feathers, cattail pollen, abalone shells, and taught how to use these in medicine practice (though I should point out that Mescalero medicine people do not make use of entheogens, unless they happen to also belong to the Native American Church). I use these sacred objects in my ritual because these are the gifts and

instructions that my teachers gave me and they have meaning for me.

Despite giving me particular gifts, instructions, and permission, *all* of my medicine teachers at Mescalero stressed that ultimately each person must find his or her own way. All medicine people within any given culture, while using common symbols, objects, and ritual actions, all have their own particular understanding of these things and have developed their own authentic relationship to them.

An authentic medicine person is creative and innovative, even when working within a highly traditional context. A "fake" medicine person is someone who simply copies others without understanding what they are doing or why they do what they do. They are only "going through the motions," as my teachers would tell me. Would-be technicians of the sacred have to learn their own way, and it must be authentic for them. Otherwise, one is just "playing with power," as my teachers would say.

Every seeker comes to the sacred in his or her own way, and there is no one way for everyone. One of my medicine teachers considered the Native American Church and its use of peyote as "imaginary" religion. It didn't speak to his authenticity (though I would also point out that he had no personal experience with entheogens). Another teacher was a member of the Native American Church, and

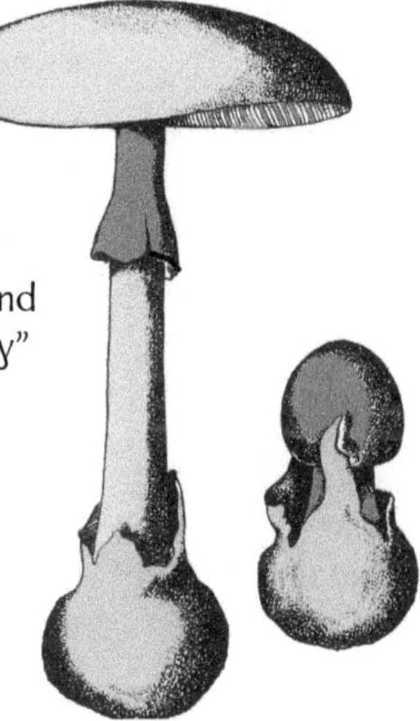

while I have never eaten peyote, when we "compared notes" on peyote and mushrooms, we found that we were coming from the same place of authenticity. It's different for everyone, and that's the way it should be.

So there is no need for anyone to try to copy someone else in creating one's sense of ritual and spiritual practice with mushrooms or other entheogens. All humans have the capacity to become a creative ritual artist, so all spiritual seekers would be advised to put their creativity to work. We should find what has meaning and significance for us. We need to find what kind of structure provides the boundaries that we need to make our experience effective. If we do it with honesty and integrity, everything will work out. As spiritual seekers, we must trust in ourselves and our integrity.

Personal Practice

I WOULD LIKE TO SHARE A LITTLE of my own practice when working with mushrooms, but I must emphasize that this is what I do because it is meaningful and significant for me. This is not intended as direct instructions for anyone else, as each seeker must find one's own way.

> Before I take mushrooms, I always bless them. This helps me set my intention and puts me into that state of mind where I acknowledged that what I am doing is serious and is not a game.

My use of ritual tends to be rather simple. I don't personally have a need to make a big, complex production out of it, though I'm not opposed to more elaborate procedures. Basically, I use ritual to set my intention and provide a clear structure for the experience. I have a beginning, middle, and end. I think of it like a frame. It gives me boundaries that I know how to work with and helps me set my mind and heart in the place I want them to be.

Before I take mushrooms, I always bless them. This helps me set my intention and puts me into that state of mind where I acknowledged that what I am doing is serious and is not a game. I treat the mushrooms as sacred, and because I do so, they are sacred.

My method of blessing the mushrooms follows techniques that I learned from my Mescalero medicine teachers, but using my own elements. I use the personal contents of my "medicine bag" to bless the mushrooms. I set up my "altar" with the objects in my medicine bag and then I bless the mushrooms with pollen from the four directions. Pollen, the four directions, and other elements of my medicine bag have meaning for me because of both the instruction I have received from my teachers and also because they resonate with my own personal experience and understanding.

After blessing them, I always let the mushrooms know what I am doing and why I am taking them. I might do this silently or I may speak to them. If I do speak, I make sure that my words are coming from my heart and from my honesty and integrity. I try my best to focus my mind and my intentions. I tell the mushrooms that I am open to anything that they have to teach me, and if they have nothing to teach me, then that's fine too. I go into the experience with intention, but not expectations. I am not attached to an end goal or product. Wherever the mushrooms take me is fine. I trust that I will learn what I need to learn. That trust has *never* been misplaced.

I go into the experience with intention, but not expectations. I am not attached to an end goal or product.

When I shake my rattle, it tells me things. It gives me information. It has different voices in it.

I will also bless and cleanse myself, and if others are participating, I will do them as well, if they desire. For this I might use sage, an eagle or hawk feather, pollen, or anything else that might seem appropriate. Even water and air will do. If there are others, I will let them hear my own intentions and will encourage them to set theirs, but I have no desire to tell others what to do or say. They have to find their own way into their experience. I will give advice, if asked, but I strongly feel that each person must be left alone to find one's path. I give assistance and guidance if requested, but otherwise I am silent.

What comes next in my ritual depends on what my intentions are, who I'm with, and what needs to be done. If I'm by myself, I might make a space to sit quietly and meditate through the experience, using my ritual tools as necessary. Or I may go out into nature and find myself there. If I am with others, I need to decide if there is someone who is requesting help. If so, I will do what I can to work with them. Ultimately, every situation is different and I try to be open to what comes and strive to learn from my experience. I don't want to waste my mushroom experience and I seek to use it wisely.

Objects of Power

ANY RITUAL TOOL CAN BE A "POWER OBJECT." A tool of mine that I have come to have particular respect for is a rattle that I have been using the past couple of years. When I shake my rattle, it tells me things. It gives me information. It has different voices in it. I listen carefully with closed eyes and I'll shake it as long as needed to sort through the different voices and find the one that I need to listen to most.

Objects of power and ritual action are always personal.

When a deep level of relationship is generated with power objects, they may come to have a life of their own.

It doesn't need to be a rattle, however. I can use a drum, or my didjeridu, or flute, or anything, really. I like my rattle, however. It has power in it and I can understand its voices.

I can also use my rattle to "drive" the experience. The rattle can help me shape the wave of the mushrooms. It helps me to "get inside" things and penetrate through their multifaceted layers and patterns. But it is just a tool. There's nothing magical about my rattle. It's just a rattle. But it is *my* tool, and I like to use it.

Objects of power and ritual action are always personal. Practitioners need to develop a relationship with their power objects and use them accordingly. As my medicine teachers told me, any object can be used in ritual as the important thing is how the practitioners uses and understands such objects. In this sense, there is no more or less powerful object from a purely practical perspective. Of course, practitioners will take into consideration objects of particular cultural and traditional relevance, or perceived physical or metaphysical properties of objects, but in theory, any object can be just as good as any other. The key is that practitioners need to explore the relationship with their power objects—something is greatly increased when power objects are made or procured in a way that recognizes their sacred role. For some, that means not letting anyone else touch personal power objects. For others it may mean taking power objects out into nature and cleansing or dedicating them. In the end, it comes down to personal preference for how such objects are to be used.

When a deep level of relationship is generated with power objects, they may come to have a life of their own. Their use in ritual may evoke detailed intuitions for action. For some, objects speak to them—not necessarily in language, but they communicate nonetheless. One might simply "just know" what do with a particular power object or how to use it for the best results, given the nature of the situation that presents itself.

Dedication

ANOTHER IMPORTANT PART of my ritual practice with mushrooms is my sense of dedication to the experience. One way that I dedicate myself is I neither eat nor drink while experiencing mushrooms, unless I really need to do so. I fast or eat only a very little the day I plan to eat mushrooms. While this may be a little extreme, and it does cause me some hardship, I do it because that is one of the ways that I help myself to take the experience seriously. I make an agreement with myself that I will not drink any water until I've passed through the experience, unless I *really* need the water. I'm not going to let myself get dehydrated or put myself in danger, but I will put up with some strong thirst. It helps me to remember to be serious about what I'm doing. And as a practical consideration, the mushroom experience tends to be longer and stronger on an empty stomach and can be significantly shortened by drinking lots of water as the mushrooms are eliminated more quickly.

Words are magic and words are wonderful, but they're also deceptions and illusions.

Another aspect of this sense of dedication might be something as simple as walking. I have found that various forms of movement help me access information. Sometimes I sway back and forth, or I may dance with the wind if I'm outside. Other times I walk. Sometimes I walk for hours, even to the point that I might end up limping around and exhausted. I don't do this because I want to suffer, but because I know that the walking helps me focus and keeps the momentum of the mushroom wave going. When I walk, I want to see the journey through to the end. I'm not going to stop until I reach the conclusion. If that means getting worn out and uncomfortable, then I'm more than willing to put up with it because I find it to be effective and rewarding. I do it because I find value in it as a tool.

Silence, Words, and Sound

SILENCE IS ANOTHER IMPORTANT PART of my ritual experience. Words are magic and words are wonderful, but they're also deceptions and illusions. When I eat mushrooms, I strive to choose my words carefully and only speak when absolutely necessary. Not only does this help me quiet my mind and to free me from my illusions, but it also helps prevent me from projecting my illusions onto others and entrapping them in my own personal drama. If I do say something, I want it to be from my heart. I want my words to be filled with honesty, integrity, and intention. I don't make idle chatter or casual references to what I see or experience. In fact, I generally won't talk about my experience until it is all through, if at all.

In contrast, many accounts of people under the influence of mushrooms detail an effluence of chanting, language, and even glossolalia. Often, these are from anthropological accounts, such as those concerning Maria Sabina, the famous Mazatec mushroom shaman. A crucial difference here is that shamans speak with the authority of the mushrooms. It is very easy to see, for example, that when Maria Sabina speaks, she is making proclamations of the mushrooms themselves. In this sense, the words are coming from a source beyond her and are not necessarily her own linguistic constructions. The significance of this is that their source in "otherness" creates a sense of authority and removes the shaman from the personal traps of language, such as projection, obfuscation, or deception. This is the language of the mushrooms, and not the shaman herself.

Songs not only invoke spirits, but they also carry messages between worlds and can profoundly affect participants in a shamanic session.

Some neo-mushroom shamans hold ceremonies where participants are invited to take their turn speaking, singing, or chanting during the course of the communal experience. When one participant speaks, all others listen. There might also be an opportunity for participants to describe their experiences at the conclusion of the ritual.

At certain stages of the mushroom experience, communication through language might be impossible, or seemingly so. At other times, words can pour forth from one with an eloquence and beauty that is enchanting. But often, the most meaningful and moving experiences come in the moments of silence, when there is just immediate knowing, intuition, and empathic understanding.

Sound is also a driving force of the entheogen experience. Shamans use sound, songs, and chants to invoke and evoke archetypal forces, spirits, and energies. Singing and chanting play central roles in most traditional shamanic work. Songs not only invoke spirits, but they also carry messages between worlds and can profoundly affect participants in a shamanic session.

Mushrooms, like other entheogens, respond readily to sounds. Repetitive rhythms and droning instruments can catapult visionaries into other realms or help them commune with transpersonal forces and dimensions. Other intelligences can also appear to communicate through sound, such as speaking through a drum, rattle, or didjeridu, even residing within the sound itself, manifesting through the very vibration.

Given that our experience of the world is made of patterns, we can also think of the world as made out of different kinds of vibrations, as vibrations are manifestations of patterns of change in space-time. Because of this vibratory nature of reality, manipulation of sound and sonic vibrations allow one to "tune in" to other frequencies and vibrations. The basic nature of vibrations is that they communicate information—all patterns are forms of information. Thus tuning in to other vibrations opens the visionary up to all kinds of information in the forms of empathy, intuition, and revelations. This can also transport the visionary into other places, other times, and other dimensions, or bring elements from these other realms back into the consensual life-world.

Reaching the End

HOW DOES ONE END THE RITUAL? For myself, I always take inventory at the conclusion of my experience. I review in my mind what I experienced, what my reactions where, how my emotional state was and is. Generally, I make such reviews a periodic part of my experience and not just at the end. Insights and revelations can come quickly,

> I thank the mushrooms for sharing their wisdom with me. I thank them for all that they have shown me. I thank them for helping me to clean out my heart and for assisting me in the ongoing challenge of letting Spirit flow freely through me.

and unless I take time to carefully review what has occurred, the insights might be lost, much like how dream images quickly dissolve upon awakening.

At the conclusion of the experience, as the last vestiges of the mushroom waves are washing over me, I take the time to assess what I have learned and what kinds of experiences I've been through on that particular journey. I look into my heart and see if I've cleaned it out. I check my honesty and my integrity. I review the lessons that I have learned and take stock of where I need to go from there. And if I have made any transgressions, I forgive myself. I don't get caught in the judgment and blame.

My usual method for this concluding review is to smoke an herbal cigarette that I rolled before the experience began. That is my way of letting myself be released from the experience and the heavy requirements that come with it. The mix of sage and osha root puts me into a moment of prayerful reverence and contemplation. I offer the cigarette to the four directions and then I smoke it. As I do, I let my lessons sink in. I thank the mushrooms for sharing their wisdom with me. I thank them for all that they have shown me. I thank them for helping me to clean out my heart and for assisting me in the ongoing challenge of letting Spirit flow freely through me. I recognize the powers around me and all the forces that have played a part in the lessons of the journey and all that they have imparted. I give thanks for the great organic unity of all existence and the guiding intelligence that exists in all things that is Spirit.

That concluding smoke is a symbol for me. It is a symbol that I have brought the experience to a conclusion as I am transitioning back into my ordinary consciousness. If I choose to talk about my experience, it will be after I finish my smoke. If I want to drink water, it is after. If I want to eat something, it is after. It is my symbol that I can relax as I've finished the work I set out to do.

Symbolic Reality

As one becomes more skilled in working with mushrooms and recognizing the aspects of one's experience, the spiritual seeker might, come to see nearly *everything* as a symbol. The way clouds blow across the surface of the moon can be a symbol, or a feather lying on one's path. They way a tree grows expresses its character and symbolizes its deeper truths. The way one sets a book on a table means volumes. Meaning abounds and symbols and signs are everywhere, especially in coincidences or unexpected moments.

Learning the ways of symbols is one of the most effective ways one can work with mushrooms due to their inherent power, and their independence from the constraints of articulated language. Symbols can be pure manifestations of Spirit, and they can also be manifestations of our illusions. Learning to work with them and understand them is learning to work with power.

Chapter 11, Main Points:

* Ritual provides a structure for actions and induces a clear mindset. It provides a safety net of structure that allows participants to know and anticipate what is happening and what is coming next. They allow one to begin, experience, and end different phases of your journey.

* Spiritual seekers should have confidence in their own innate capacity to connect to and create the sacred. Humans are ritual-creating beings. Rituals make use of our natural state of being as pattern-manifesting reality creators and structure it, give it meaning, and connect us with the sacred.

CHAPTER 12

Symbols

Symbols are everywhere, all the time. Symbols can be seen as representations of patterns. They are the concrescences of our life patterns. Symbols carry within them all of the depth of our experience, our emotions, our thoughts, and our desires. They can represent us or connect us to other realities or ways of being. They are power. When working with them, the spiritual seeker works with power. Symbols can reveal information to the mushroom eater and they can change or challenge one's experience. Recognizing and working with symbols is a fundamental aspect of working with mushrooms.

What are our symbols? Anything can be a symbol, and in fact, most things as we experience them, are symbols. Because we exist in a constantly flowing and changing reality of patterns of manifestations, symbols stand as a fixed and relatively stable embodiment of those patterns. In other words, understanding a symbol gives

You are never the same after you've had the veil drawn.

Archetypes are powerful, universal, and transcendent symbols.

insight into the pattern of which it is a concrescence. Symbols help us navigate and make sense of our constantly changing experience. Though they may appear to be fixed and stable, this is only relatively so, and one's understanding of and relationship to symbols change over time. They tend to be more stable than not, however, and therefore if one can access the depth of the symbol, the spiritual seeker can get the to the heart of the pattern far more easily than without the symbol.

Archetypes and Concrescences

THE MOST POWERFUL, UNIVERSAL, AND TRANSCENDENT symbols are called "archetypes." These are understood to represent universal aspects of human experience and there have been numerous studies and writings on the nature of archetypes. In religious or spiritual terms, the most powerful archetypes are seen as concrescences of the sacred.

What is a "concrescence?" Methaporically, I think of this term in relationship to quantum physics. In quantum physics, there is the concept of the quantum wave function. The wave function addresses the dual nature of sub-atomic reality as existing simultaneously as both particles and waves. The quantum world is a strange one. At best, we can only describe it as a nebulous nexus of possibilities and probabilities. The wave function is a mathematical description of the range of probabilities for any quantum system or "object." Before a quantum system is observed, physicists can only speak of waves of probability. However, when they actually observe a quantum system, the act of observing "collapses" the wave function and the quantum system then "appears" as a wave or a particle. There are all kinds of philosophical disagreements over what this means relative to the nature of reality and the possible effects of consciousness on physical objects—but there's no need for us to get into this debate.

However, there is an interesting metaphor here that is heuristically useful. When the probability wave of a quantum system is observed, an "object" can suddenly and almost magically appear. This "object" is a "concrescence" of the probability pattern of a wave. One can think of symbols the same way. A symbol is an object, icon, image, concept, or state that is the concrescence of a deeper pattern of probabilities and possibilities. Working with the symbol therefore gives spiritual seekers access to the concrescence of patterns it represents—just as a physicist making an observation can learn something of the nature of a quantum system. Often this is experienced as profound moments of revelation within the entheogen experience.

Explaining the use and function of symbols is most easily done by using examples. Everyone has their own symbols and we use them in different ways. There is no one map to understanding or using symbols, for every person is different and we all have different symbols. Symbols reflect both the uniqueness, and the universal qualities, of individuals. They are simultaneously universal archetypes and personal concrescences of a person's spiritual state and experience.

The Woman from NASA

To illustrate how recognition of symbols, and their significance, can take place in mushroom experiences, consider the following personal story.

Symbols give spiritual seekers access to the concrescence of patterns they represent.

At a Burning Man art festival, my camp mates and I ate some mushrooms one night and then went out onto the playa with the intention of spiritually exploring the art. We got caught at an incomplete work of art for various reasons. It consisted of a metal arch from which was suspended an empty frame that swung about freely in the breeze.

I watched as a couple came up to the metal frame. The man played with the frame, but the woman approached it very cautiously and then, almost fearfully, backed away. Curious about their reactions, I asked the man, "How was it?" He gave a quick and playful answer, dancing around me as though I were the frame. I then turned to the woman.

To my surprise, she instantly became very nervous. I could visibly see her shaking. Because she was so nervous I smiled and extended out my hand. When she noticed what I had done, she placed her hand in mind. I then put my other hand on top of hers and she did likewise. There we stood, holding each other's hands in the middle of the night with the wind blowing from behind me and playa dust pelting against us.

We stood in near-total silence for probably thirty minutes or more with only a few brief exchanges of words.

She gripped my hands tightly as she stood there in silence, shaking in the wind. I could literally feel her fear and anxiety. It felt like she was holding onto my hands for dear life. Despite how much she wanted to let go, she couldn't. My intuition was that she was afraid to accept her own spirit.

Earlier that day I had seen a golden eagle fly over our camp. As I held her hands in mine, I could feel the wind blowing between our hands and fingers. Her hands felt to me like eagle wings. I saw her as a fledgling eagle that was too afraid to spread her wings and take that first tentative flight out of the nest. That was why she was holding on so tightly.

She tried to fight the fear. She took deep breaths, centered herself, and tried to relax. She only allowed herself a few brief moments to relax her grip, however, and she would quickly regain her tight hold, too fearful to let go.

Eventually I decided that it was time for me to speak the words the mushrooms were urging me to say. I leaned over and quietly whispered in her ear, "Don't forget to fly."

The woman's reaction was immediate. "I've always wanted to fly!" she blurted out. "But I've been so afraid!" she quickly added.

It was then that I noticed for the first time, and perhaps even she too, that she was wearing a blue NASA flight suit. "But you're wearing a NASA flight suit," I commented

She looked down at herself in near shock. She was wearing her fear right there on her very body. She had wrapped herself in her desire for a soaring spirit but was afraid to let it go. She was wearing the symbol that was most important to her and she barely even knew it. The woman was convinced that I was reading her mind and even asked me if I was psychic. All that was happening was that I was seeing her through the symbols that manifested her inner spirit, her fears, her dreams, and her desire to free herself from her self-imposed limits. Clearly, she had some looking in the spiritual mirror to do.

I had seen a golden eagle fly over our camp.

In mushroom consciousness, this was a perfectly ordinary experience. Symbols are everywhere, all the time, showing the state of our spirit and that of those around us.

Susan was a Pyramid

ANOTHER INTERESTING PERSONAL EXAMPLE comes from a mushroom experience with a couple I'll call Jeff and Susan. What transpired was a very powerful mushroom session of working with symbols.

As the mushrooms were just beginning to come on, I felt that we needed a space in which to work. Their living room was big and spacious. I moved a table out of the way and cleared out a space on the rug.

I wandered outside and picked a flowering dandelion from the lawn in front of their house and took it inside where I placed it at the center of the rug. Under the influence of the growing mushroom consciousness, the little yellow flower was the light of Spirit that shines in the center of all of us.

When Susan saw the flower on the rug she proclaimed, "Let's all put something on the rug!", then hurried off to her bedroom. Soon she returned with a small, darkly colored pyramid that she placed on the rug next to the flower.

As Susan sat looking at the pyramind I walked in circles around the edge of the rug, observing the situation until I was overcome with the urge to change it. Without speaking, I tipped the pyramid onto its side, which had a powerful and immediate affect upon Susan. Even though she was sitting on the floor, Susan tipped over too—she *was* the pyramid.

I circled around the rug a little longer. I became overwhelmed with the desire to break something. I just knew that *something* needed to be broken.

I searched through the house, looking for something completely irrelevant, something that wouldn't upset my friends if I broke it. In the kitchen, I found a generic drinking glass. I held it. No emotional resonance there. This would do.

I took the glass into the living room. I didn't want to break it on the rug, so I grabbed a nearby newspaper and placed the glass on it to catch the soon-to-be-produced shards.

To break the glass I felt the need for something primal, something unformed, something completely and utterly basic and simple. I went into the back yard where I found a big moss-covered rock. This would do. I took the rock back in the house and smashed it down on the glass. Susan immediately burst into tears.

I wanted something to put the broken pieces of glass in, so I went looking about until I found the right object—a small bowl. As I collected the shards of glass and placed them in the bowl, Susan, still crying, went to her bedroom where she continued to cry.

Later, after the waning of our mushroom experience, I learned that Susan had identified with the little pyramid for years. She said that my tipping the pyramid had been a profound moment for her because she had never considered placing the pyramid on its side, so that when I tipped it over, it fundamentally altered her perception of the pyramid—and of herself. She said that she suddenly saw herself and her life from a perspective she had never before contemplated. The pyramid was the symbolic focus of Susan's experience and my altering it had a profound

> The pyramid was the symbolic focus of her experience. When I tipped it over she suddenly saw her life from a perspective she had never before contemplated.

Don't let others interpret your symbols, for that is filtering the experience through language, and through another person's experience of those symbols.

symbolic effect on her. Interestingly, Susan also had an attachment to the little bowl that I used to hold the broken glass.

In preparation for the mushroom session, Susan indicated that she was seeking a spiritual realization. She didn't know where to look for it, however. Susan talked of spending time in the desert, or going off to seek enlightenment. Perhaps what she really needed was a change in perspective.

A few months later, Susan divorced Jeff and went on a journey to "discover" herself. She joined a band—something she had never done before—and she made a piligrimage to the desert.

Susan's symbols communicated to her the need for a rather difficult reorganization of herself and her life. When she looked at herself from a different perspective, contemplating the source of Spirit, she found her sense of identity shattered, which she had to struggle to put back together. She was on the precipice of change and likely the mushroom session of working with symbols played a key role in her subsequent decision to leave Jeff to seek a new personal path.

The Language of Symbols

WORKING WITH SYMBOLS is not the same as explaining them with language. Language is removed from the actual experience. Trying to articulate the significance of symbols through language is partially successful, at best. Let the symbol speak for itself. Spiritual seekers are wise to explore their personal meaning of symbols encountered during the mushroom experience.

Don't let others interpret your symbols, for that is filtering the experience through language, and through another person's experience of those symbols. We can listen to the interpretations of others when they offer particular insight, but we are the ones who must decide what our symbols mean for us and our life.

Symbols are powerful, in part, because they transcend the limits and constrictions of language and interpreted narrative. Symbols have the power to affect us directly, unmediated through the filter of language and rational thought. In this way, they impact our experience of them, especially when in the mushroom state. Symbols have the ability to make realizations of patterns direct and immediate. When they are worked with consciously and with intention, they can empower us to transcend.

Anything can be a symbol. All we need to do is look around us to find them. A symbol needn't be a physical object. It can be the way one always stubs the same toe. It can be the small grunt one makes when thinking a self-critical thought. It can be the way objects are arranged in one's living space. It can be something you experienced in a dream, or a piece of art. Or it could be the way a bird flies across the sky, or the provocative twist of a tree branch, or the peculiar character of a room or place.

Discovering personal symbols is like a game. It takes insight and thought. Spiritual seekers discover personal symbols by contemplating what they think and perceive about themselves and their lives. Chances are, they will

Discovering personal symbols is a voyage of discovery.

Understanding how symbols evoke feelings of empathy, intuition, and revelation is a major aspect of working with them.

find many more symbols than they had imagined. It is a voyage of discovery. Spiritual seekers can take a journey into themselves to see what symbols they have collected to mark their way.

When spiritual seekers learn to recognize symbols, they can learn to work with them. Symbols are tools that open up various kinds of spiritual experiences and realizations. Symbols are fluid and changing. How we perceive and work with symbols changes from day to day, experience to experience. When they find the symbols that represent things they'd like to change or learn more of, spiritual seekers explore them to find their richness and depth and what they reveal about their lives. Similarly, when we find symbols that are powerful and spiritually resonant for ourselves, we, as spiritual practitioners, can learn to use them effectively in our personal spiritual work.

Perhaps most importantly, when we learn how to work with personal symbols, we learn how to look into our hearts and take care of what we find there so that Spirit may flow freely through our being.

Empathy and Intuition

UNDERSTANDING HOW SYMBOLS EVOKE feelings of empathy, intuition, and revelation is a major aspect of working with them. This is true when working on oneself, and perhaps even more so when working with others, as the cases above illustrate.

Empathy plays a major role in my experiences with mushrooms, especially when others are involved. When we explore the symbols that are important to others, strong empathic feelings are often evoked, leading to various intuitions and revelations regarding words, actions, and further use of symbols. This is what led the "woman from NASA" to wonder if I were "psychic." When the empathic understanding flows in the mushroom experience, I find that the hearts and minds of others become open and accessible to a profound degree. We can get inside the feelings of another to actually feel their pain in our own body and mind, understanding their roots, causes, and means of expression.

> Shamans invite the spirits and symbols to work through them for the purpose of helping others.

Often the contemplation of the symbols significant to others evokes this kind of experience, though it is augmented by movement, observation, and physical touch. Using intuition and listening to the revelations of the mushrooms, shamanic relationships are created that open explorers up to healing and self-discovery.

An important key to engaging in such work is for those practicing in a shamanic role to get their ego-based sense of self out of the way. Those who would strive to work with others in this capacity need to work with symbols and empathic experience from a stance that is not involved in the ego-driven desires of the one doing the work so that they may approach others from a place of authenticity and integrity. It is not about manipulating others, but working with them to empower them through their own symbols and personal understandings of themselves. There is a great different between getting inside the hearts and minds of others for their benefit and doing so out of personal desires.

Embodiment and Shapeshifting

MANY SHAMANS ACCOMPLISH the goal of getting the ego out of the way by taking on different personas when shamanizing, often in the form of shapeshifting. For those who are open to the experience, symbols can be embodied and actualized in one's body, creating cognitive, behavioral, and even physically-experienced changes. Such changes allow shamans to approach others from a place of authority and personal neutrality. Shamans invite the spirits and symbols to work through them for the purpose of helping others in any capacity that they may need. This is not about the ego-driven desires of the shaman, but rather is about getting the self out of the way so that Spirit may flow through and do its work. It's about using the embodiment of symbols and shapeshifting to be a conduit for transcendent powers.

Shapeshifting can be experienced in a variety of ways. At lower doses of mushrooms, visionaries may experience themselves as merging with objects, images, or the imaginal content of their visions. At higher doses, profound changes take place in the sensation of one's body, and shamans might feel themselves taking on the physical characteristics of a symbol or, very commonly, of a nature spirit in the form of an animal, plant, bird, or natural landform or object. At the highest doses, this may involve a complete out-of-body experience where shamans feel their spirit completely leaving their physical form and transforming into another being in the hyper-dimensional visionary space.

When shamans shapeshift, they transport themselves into the world of archetypes where symbols are coupled to highly provocative powers and intuitive abilies.

When shamans shapeshift, they transport themselves into the world of archetypes where symbols are coupled to highly provocative powers and intuitive abilies. Courses of action become immediately apparent as do words that must be spoken, symbols used, or sounds produced. The actions and deeds of the shaman then have a profound effect on others who are participating in the shamanic encounter, bring others to deep states of realization, healing, and empowerment.

Experienced shamans have a repertoire of spirits and transformative symbols that they evoke and invoke in their work with others called helping spirits, spirit allies, power animals. The basic idea is that through the psycho-somatic transformation, the shaman is better able to manifest the transcendent powers of these archetypal energies in the life-world of the patient or person seeking help or healing.

Chapter 12, Main Points:

* Symbols carry within them all of the depth of our experience, our emotions, our thoughts, and our desires.

* While some symbols, such as archetypes, tend to have universal implications, many symbols are highly individual, like people.

* Symbols are concrescences of our life-patterns. Working with symbols gives us access to the system of patterns it is a manifestation of.

* Let symbols speak for themselves, and seek to find your own meaning. Don't let others interpret your symbols for you. Listen to them if you think they have insight, but you are the one who must decide what your symbols mean for you and your own life and experience.

* Working with symbols is working with power.
* Working with symbols evokes feelings of empathy, intuition, and revelation.
* Shapeshifting and embodiment of symbols is a method for becoming an open conduit for transcendent powers.

CHAPTER 13

The Clean Heart

HAVING A CLEAN HEART is a fundamental goal of working spiritually with mushrooms. Looking into the spiritual mirror is a way of getting into one's heart to deal with what one finds there. The heart is where we carry emotions, wounds, pain. It's the window to joy and pleasure. It is the seat of our emotions. Emotions are our reactions to what we think, do, believe, and encounter in the world.

> . . . Under the full force of mushrooms, the heavens open up with a display of beauty hard to describe. Visual acuity is enhanced to the point where the sky becomes three dimensional. The distances between stars and galaxies appear obvious. Electromagnetic fields ebb and flow . . . Overlaying this display of splendor are colorful, dancing, geometrical fractals of infinite complexity. The universe moves in harmony. My spirit moves with it. I feel as though I have become a thread in the fabric of nature and have returned home.
>
> -- Paul Stamets

If our actions are beyond reproach and we have intimate knowledge of ourselves, then our hearts are clean. There is no need for self-judgment or the spiraling cycles of depression and criticism that we so easily fall into. When your heart is clean, there is no need for you to hurt or abuse others in word, deed, or thought. Why? Because the clean heart is at peace. Having a clean heart is the ideal state, for when our hearts are clean, we can live at peace with ourselves. When we live at peace with our self, we are at peace with the world and all that we find in it.

The Heart of Peace

THE HEART OF PEACE is the heart of love and compassion. This is the most basic state of Spirit. Spirit does not judge and it does not condemn. As much as we might like to think that some divine judge will reward or punish us for our actions, we are the real judges. When we are condemned, it is our self that is the judge. Pure, flowing Spirit is compassion and love. Why? Because there is no difference. At the deepest core, your heart and the heart of the universe are one and the same. That means that all hearts are connected to the heart of the universe. And certainly, the universe is at peace with itself.

Spirit does not judge and it does not condemn.

The heart of the universe is filled with love, compassion, and the pure joy of creative expression and the continual striving for further creation. The heart of the universe continually seeks to make the possible the actual and strives for the ongoing expression and development of the infinite complexity and richness of the phenomenal world. The heart of the universe is filled with creative passion, and it seeks vessels and means for its fullest expression.

All Things Contained Therein

I THINK OF MY HEART AS A CONTAINER. Looking into my heart is like looking into that container. When I have negative emotional resonances, which are my reactions to my thoughts and experiences, the inside of the container of my heart becomes incrusted with negative emotions. These negative emotions attach to my heart much like my arteries would get clogged from a poor diet and lack of exercise. The longer we let emotional resonances in our heart lay unresolved, the more the wound festers. The crust on my heart gets thicker. When that happens, the free flow of Spirit from the heart of the universe is constricted. The more constricted the heart, the more we live in our own illusions. We get caught in our self-generated dramas of pain and blame. We punish ourselves and we punish others. The clean heart has no need to punish, because the free flow of Spirit is love, compassion, and creativity.

This well of creativity at the heart of the universe is very difficult to describe. All things are contained therein. All the pleasure, all the pain, the joys, the suffering. There, in the heart that binds all things together, both pleasure and pain, joy and suffering, lightness and darkness are transcended by the pure flow of creative energy. It is creativity that binds all things in the universe together in one great cosmic symphony, continually striving, continually creating, and always seeking further expression and novelty, simply for the sake of creativity. The manifest universe is the great creative dream of Spirit, unfolding in the fabric of space and time.

The clean heart has no need to punish, because the free flow of Spirit is love, compassion, and creativity.

Emotional Resonance

THE HEART IS THE CORE OF OUR EMOTIONS, because emotions are a resonance, a vibration. The pattern of the emotion affects us at all levels of our being. It is useful to think of our self as having an emotional body. Depending on our experience, we might think of this as contiguous with the physical body or not—it depends on what we experience. In this sense, our experience of our bodies can tell us about our emotions. This is why I appreciate the fact that I can *feel* the mushrooms working their way through my body. As they move through my body, they force me to experience different physical sensations, to access different emotions as they resonate in different patterns through my emotional body.

Using our body in different ways opens up or closes off different emotions.

Learning about the body is learning about emotions. Using our body in different ways opens up or closes off different emotions. Movement, massage, chanting, imaginal shape-shifting, all help us to access different aspects of our body and the emotional resonances stored in our psycho-physical beings.

Spiritual seekers are wise to get to know their bodies. When one experiences mushrooms, there is a radical reorientation of the notion of the self as it is related to the body. Mushroom eaters have an entirely different experience of body to explore and come to know. When spiritual seekers learn how their bodies react to, interact with, and yes, *embody* symbols, they learn how to really get at their emotions and understand them. When they understand their emotions, spiritual seekers can release them, transform them, or if need be, heal them.

Just as there is depth to the body, so too is there depth to emotions. Certain vibrations are more "surface" whereas others are closer to the heart. Often going directly to the heart is difficult as that's where the most powerful emotional resonances are found. To get there spiritual seekers may have to deal with multiple more surface layers, slowly working to the very heart. It may take several, or many, sessions to really get to the heart, but if spiritual seekers are patient and dedicated, they will get there, and that's when they can really clean the heart out.

Continual Striving

I CAN FEEL THE FREE FLOW OF SPIRIT when my heart is clean. I can really express myself and be who and what I truly am, not the things I think I should be or the projections I want to create of myself or others. When my heart is clean, enthusiasm and creativity flow through me. I use that flow. I shape it, ride with it, and let it carry me along. What I do and what I say and feel is authentic for me and who and what I am. I am at peace with myself and what I am doing and my relationships with others.

I can feel the free flow of Spirit when my heart is clean.

Is this true 100% of the time? Honestly, no. I, like anyone else, need continual maintenance. I need to return to my heart and look into it and deal honestly with what I find. I, like everyone else, make mistakes, pass judgment, and criticize myself. I get caught up in dramas. I hurt the ones I love. I treat myself disrespectfully. I become the victim and the judge. I get angry. I do things and say things I regret later. But I know I can return to my heart, look at it honestly, and deal with what I find there. When I get off the path, I take the time to go inside and see what I find there. When I'm strong, I can deal with what I find honestly and with integrity. If I'm feeling weak, I might cower and try too hard.

What is important is not whether I succeed or not, but that I strive—strive to keep my heart clean, strive to be honest with myself, strive to let Spirit flow freely through me, strive to get my own illusions of myself out of the way so that my heart can feel that very real and tangible connection to the heart of the universe. Striving is what counts. There is no final end. There is no goal. There is only the striving and the continual return to our hearts and the truth that we find there.

Chapter 13, Main Points:

* The art of looking into the spiritual mirror is the art of looking into one's heart.

* Working with mushrooms spiritually is about cleaning out one's heart.

* The clean heart is at peace. Having a clean heart is the ideal state to be in, for when the heart is clean, the spiritual seeker lives at peace with himself. When one lives at peace with one's self, you are at peace with the world and all you find in it.

* Our hearts are connected to the heart of the universe, and the heart of the universe is filled with love, compassion, and creative joy.

* Our experience of our bodies can tell us about our emotions.

* Learning about your body is learning about your emotions. Using your body in different ways opens up or closes off access to different emotions.

* When spiritual seekers learn how their bodies react to, interact with, and *embody* symbols, they will learn how to really get at their emotions and understand them. When spiritual seekers understand their emotions, they can release them, transform them, or if need be, heal them.

* When one's heart is clean, the creative flow of Spirit can pass through you unimpeded.

CHAPTER 14

Spirit Flow

HOW CAN THERE BE A BEGINNING to spiritual experience? How can there be an end? Is there a beginning or end to the universe? There is no beginning, and there is no end. There is only the continual striving for further creation, for the further exploration of being, for the ongoing expression of the spirit of love, compassion, and creativity.

> We suspect that, in its fullest sense, the creative faculty, whether in the humanities or science or industry, that most precious of man's distinctive possessions and the one most clearly partaking of the divine, is linked in some way with the area of the mind that the mushrooms unlock
> -- Gordon Wasson

The spirit of the universe is one of love, compassion, and endless creativity. The well of love, compassion and creativity is infinite. It is not contained within either time or space and therefore is beyond any limit or boundary that we might ever imagine. But Pure Spirit is nothing without the play of the universe. The only way for

Pure Spirit to express itself and make itself known to itself is through the ongoing play of space-time. Beyond space and time nothing happens, for it is no-place and it is no-thing. There is no-thing there because there is no *there* for some-thing to exist in. It is unchanging, unchanged, and unbound.

To my mind, the Divine Imagination is the source of all creativity in our dreams, in our psychedelic experiences, in the jungles, in the currents of the ocean, and in the organization of protozoan and microbial life.
-- Terence McKenna

The Spirit of the universe is the source of what we experience as space-time. It is the source of the never-ceasing patterns of manifestation and creation, but it is not a thing, an object, or a place. It is what it is and it is no-thing.

We live in the world of things. We live in the world of superstrings and galaxies and everything in between. This is the realm of expression of the Spirit of the universe. What is this universe if not an ongoing expression of creativity? Pure Spirit uses space and time, the matrix of our phenomenal being, to express itself in creative action. "Creation," as a term to refer to the universe, is a very poor semantic choice. A far more accurate term would be "Creating."

Nothing "created" the universe. The universe is constantly being created in each and every moment. The Spirit of the universe is continually creating itself as the phenomenal world. There is no beginning to this creative play and there is no end. There is only the present moment of creative activity as the patterns that generate the phenomenal world play themselves out in intimate interconnection with each other.

Creative Identity

WHEN OUR HEARTS ARE CLEAN, our state of being is no different from the state of being of the universe. We become an active creative force in the universe. We create rituals. We create symbols. We create art. We create ourselves and the world around us. We are the universe looking back at itself. We may feel separate and isolated, but we are an expression of the source and our hearts connect us back to that source. The universe wants to see how far it can go. Where will the play of creativity take the universe? What are the limits of the possible? What are the limits of creative action?

Spiritual seekers must answer these questions for themselves. When Spirit flows through us, we cannot help but be a creative force. Creativity is the *natural* state of being. Creativity gives us joy. Creativity helps us to push our own limited sense of self aside and feel that flow of spirit come through us. Through creativity, we understand how our choices, our tools, and our methods affect our work and our ability to express. When we clean out our hearts, our creativity comes out of our authentic sense of self. It comes from a place of honesty and compassion.

When Spirit flows through us, we cannot help but be a creative force. Creativity is the natural state of being.

Art and Spirit

WHEN WE ENCOUNTER THE PRODUCTS of creativity that comes from a clean heart, we know it. Spirit speaks to us through the work. It can be a painting, a piece of music, or the way someone smiles at us, or the way a person sits or carries their body. When we experience Spirit flow we *feel* it and we *know* it.

There's a great deal of art in the world. We're surrounded by art and creative expression. Everywhere we turn there are creative forms of entertainment and creative products for us to enjoy. But there is a great difference between creativity that comes from free flowing Spirit and creativity that comes from our illusions, or limited sense of self.

This is not necessarily about the difference between religious and secular art. This is the difference between art that comes from Spirit and art that comes from our wounds, our illusions, our dramas and traps that we set for ourselves. This is also not the difference between beautiful art and ugly art, or "high" art or "low" art. This is not about art that is defined by conventional categories.

Spirit art can be anything. It can be crude or sophisticated. It can be simple or complex. What it all has is that indefinable connection to Spirit. When we experience it, we know. It's both that enigmatic and that simple. When someone speaks to us from their heart, we know it. Similarly, when we experience creativity that comes from spirit, we know. We know because our own hearts know what the free flow of Spirit is, even if we can't put it into words or explain it to anyone else, or even to ourself. When our hearts are clean and open, we just know.

Spirit art can be anything. It can be crude or sophisticated. It can be simple or complex.

Creating

THE CLOSER SPIRITUAL SEEKERS ARE to their hearts, the more creative and freely expressive they become. Their art might be dark or light, pleasant or not, but it will come from a place of knowing and from a place of honesty. It will not be caught up in dramas, though it may express them. It will be something that they can give freely to others. It may expose their hearts to others, but it will not make them self-conscious or make them feel the need to judge themselves or be concerned what others will think. If they like it, that is fine. If they don't, that is fine too. Spiritual seekers will be creative because that is how Spirit flows through them.

It is important to understand that by "creativity" I do not necessarily mean the act or experience of creating "art" as we may traditionally understand it. Experiencing nature can be a creative act. Dreaming can be a creative act. Performing our work or doing a job can be a creative act. Making music, or drawing, or working with wood or clay or making a movie are creative acts as well. The key is that in creative acts, whatever they are, that one experience the free flow of Spirit. Sometimes this will be more evident and obvious than others. Sometimes, spiritual seekers will have an immediate and intuitive understanding of what is happening and how Spirit is expressing itself. At other times it may be less so. Some creative acts have a strong flow of Spirit and some weaker. The better we are at getting our self, our fears, and our illusions out of the way, the more powerful our art will be and the more clearly the light of Spirit will shine through.

Art as Spiritual Reflection and Practice

MY STRONGEST EXPERIENCES of the free flow of Spirit have been with my experiences with mushrooms. I do not attempt to make "art" while under the influence of mushrooms, at least not in the conventional sense. Rituals can be art, as

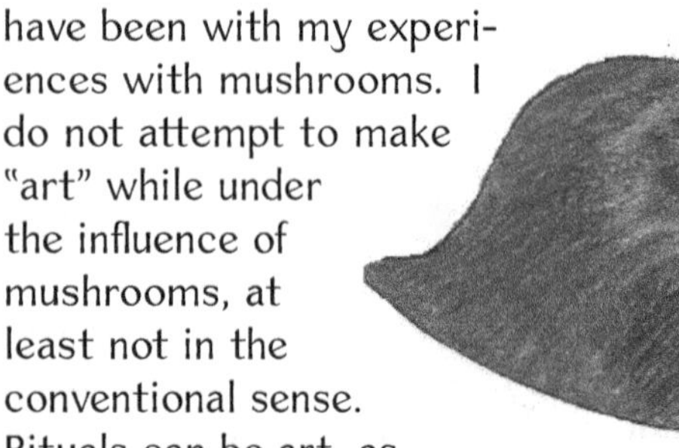

can symbols and their use. But mostly my connection to creativity is what I take from the experience that will then influence my art later, when I'm striving to create, be it writing, making music, drawing, or any other creative act I might engage in. But when I'm really in the flow of creative action, I can feel that Spirit, and I do everything I can to let it flow through me and I use that power to express myself in the purest and most honest way I can.

My art is a window through which I can look to see the state of my heart and spirit. If my art comes out all dark and clouded, I know that there's something going on inside that I need to deal with. If my art is light and filled with beauty, I know that I'm at peace inside. My art helps me to understand my own emotions and my own state of being in the world. My art is a tool to help me look in the spiritual mirror.

I don't make art for other people. I enjoy it when I know that others appreciate my art or feel that it speaks to them or inspires their creativity, but that is not why I engage in creative activities. I engage in creative activity because it connects me with that flow of Spirit, and that is a wonderful thing. I create because I want to and it gives me great pleasure. I love the act of creating. The process is itself a beautiful and fascinating thing. Naturally, I want to have an impressive product for my activity, and I want others to be impressed too, but that's just my ego talking. The genuine pleasure is from the act itself.

My art is a window through which I can look through to see the state of my heart and spirit.

Art can be healing. Expressing our spirit is the most healing thing we can do, and art of all forms is the perfect medium.

Everyone an Artist

MY HOPE FOR ALL SPIRITUAL SEEKERS is that if they have not found their source of creativity, in whatever form it may take, that they will strive with all their passion to discover it, and for all people to know that their life is a creative expression of the free flow of Spirit. We are all artists. We all have the capacity to create, to share, and to strive for the further creative expression of the universe. We are creators. We create the world around us at every moment and in every instant. May we all become conscious creators. May we be creators who come from a place of compassion, love, and pure creativity.

> Looking into the spiritual mirror, seeing into our hearts, seeing the patterns, and working with symbols is all about getting back to that place where we can experience the free flow of Spirit.

Looking into the spiritual mirror, seeing into our hearts, seeing the patterns, and working with symbols is all about getting back to that place where we can experience the free flow of Spirit. When Spirit flows, it is like a clean breeze flowing through our being. We can use it to create, to heal ourselves and others, to be a creative and compassionate force in the universe. We have the power within us to directly and actively participate in the creation of the universe. Our spirits and the Spirit of the universe are identical. There is no difference. There is no creative force that exists outside of us that does not also exist inside us. May we all tap into it. May we all make compassionate and conscious use of it. May we make ourselves and our lives works of art. We have the power, the capacity, and the ability. All we need to do is tap into it and learn to work with it.

May the spirit of the universe flow through us like the wind through an open window. May we find that peace within that comes from a clean heart and may it open us to the infinite light that always resides on the other side of the darkness of our illusions. May we be empowered to be what we are.

Chapter 14, Main Points:

* The Spirit of the universe is one of love, compassion, and endless creativity. The well of love, compassion and creativity is infinite. It is not contained within either time or space and therefore is beyond any limit or boundary that we might ever imagine.

* The Spirit of the universe is the source of what we experience as space-time.

* The Spirit of the universe is continually creating itself as the phenomenal world.

* When one's heart is clean, one's state of being is no different from the state of being of the universe. The spiritual seeker becomes an active and conscious creative force in the universe.

* The closer one is to one's own heart, the more creative and freely expressive the spiritual seeker will become. One's art might be dark or light, pleasant or not, but it will come from a place of knowing and from a place of honesty.

* Expressing one's spirit is the most healing thing one can do.

* There is no creative force that exists outside of us that does not also exist inside us.

CHAPTER 15

Final Thoughts

THE TECHNIQUES, methods, and spiritual experiences we've discussed are perhaps best described as a style of spiritual practice that combines classical elements of both shamanism and mysticism. As shamanism and mysticism share a great deal in common, but are also somewhat distinct areas of spiritual practice and experience, it is worthwhile exploring how these techniques and ideas discussed here might apply to either.

> The Gaian mind is a real mind: its messages are real messages, and our task—through discipline, dreams, psychedelics, attention to detail, whatever we have going—is to try and extract its messages and eliminate our own interference so that we can see the face of the Other and respond to what it wants.

In the literature on religion and religious experience, the category of "mystical experience" is most generally associated with well-established religions and their spiritual practices. Therefore, those who study comparative mysticism tend to look at either the similarity or dissimilarity of experiences of those steeped in classical traditions such as Buddhism, Christianity, Islam, Judaism, Hinduism, Taoism, and to some extent, other lesser-known and practiced religions. Indigenous traditions, where shamanism tends to dominate, are rarely taken into consideration by scholars of comparative mysticism, though this is changing.

The Kantian View

WITHIN THE STUDY OF MYSTICISM there are those scholars who argue for a "Kantian" approach to the subject, which is to say that both the content and interpretation of mystical experience is deemed to be completely dependent on the mystic's culture, tradition, and religious filter. In this sense, mystics have a different experience that is a product of their particular religion and understanding. Under such a view, it is possible to say that there are as many kinds of mystical experiences as there are mystics, or at the least, as many kinds of mystical experiences as there are religions or particular traditions of mystical practice within religions.

The Kantian view ultimately says that the experiences of different mystics are not alike, especially when compared across religions. Buddhists, for example, do not have mystical experiences that can be compared to the experiences of Christians, because they come from different traditions, have different concepts, different spiritual philosophies, and engage in fundamentally different practices. In more recent times, the Kantian view has been understood to indicate that all human experiences are ultimately products of culture. There is nothing fundamental out there—just human constructions of reality that are played out in cultural contexts. This is the view of the post-structuralists and postmodernists.

The Perennial Philosophy

PERENNIAL PHILOSOPHY IS A DIFFERENT APPROACH to mysticism and mystical experience. Those who accept the Perennial Philosophy argue that while there are many different religions and systems of spiritual practice, and while practitioners have a wide variety of experiences that are given different names and different interpretations, at heart, the mystical experience is ultimately one. In other words, there are many paths and many methods for arriving at an experience of the fundamental nature of being, but ultimately, they all come from and return back to the same source.

There are many paths and many methods for arriving at an experience of the fundamental nature of being.

Under this view, the basic nature of the mystical experience is transcendent of culture, time, or place. Those who have such experiences, under reflection, put the experience into a framework that is culturally meaningful and significant, using traditional terms and language, but just because people use different means to describe and communicate the experience, does not mean that the experience itself was different.

Neurobiological Mysticism

RECENT STUDIES ON THE NEUROBIOLOGY OF MYSTICISM and spiritual experience support the perennial view in that the biological structures of the brain allow for certain kinds of experience. We may all have different cultures and religions, but brain structure is universally human.

Our physical limits and biological nature plays a direct role in the kinds of experiences that we may have as physical and conscious beings. Philosophically, this is a weak form of determinism because our experience is not completely determined by brain structure or neurochemistry, but there are certain limits or ranges of experiences that are influenced by these physical aspects of our brains.

The neurobiological approach to mysticism is more relevant when enthoegenic substances such as mushrooms are involved. Mushrooms belong to the class of tryptamine psychedelics, which have been called "neurotransmitter" plants. This is because the active components of mushrooms, as well as ayahuasca, LSD, and DMT, are all chemically related to naturally occurring neurotransmitters in the human brain, and are in fact also closely related to the secretions of the pineal gland, which is often called the "third eye" by both mystics and brain scientists becasue the pineal gland seems to be closely associated with higher states of consciousness.

The result is that when one consumes psilocybin mushrooms or other tryptamine substances, one is taking in substances that directly affect the brain and the way that the brain processes information. Given that all of our experience of reality is the product of chemical reactions in the brain, the world as experienced under tryptamines is just a different mental construct.

When one consumes psilocybin mushrooms or other tryptamine substances, one is taking in substances that directly affect the brain and the way that the brain processes information.

It's All in Your Mind

THOSE OPPOSED TO HALLUCINOGENS argue that "it's all in your mind." This comment is generally made in a dismissive manner, indicating that the contents of psychedelic experience are fundamentally imaginary or unreal. However, the argument can just as easily go the other way, because our ordinary experiences of reality are a product of chemicals in the brain as well, and there is no necessary philosophical reason to judge that one is "more real" than the other.

> In the mushroom state, there is no subject, no object. There is only the basic suchness of being.

There may not be a good philosophical reason for believing that one state of consciousness is more real than another, but there is the experiential argument. A common judgment of those who consume mushrooms is the belief that what they experience and perceive in the mushroom state is fundamentally more real and authentic than what they experience in ordinary states of consciousness, even while recognizing its fantastical nature.

Beyond Logic

THIS CANNOT BE ARGUED LOGICALLY. It is simply a fundamental truth of the experience. When one has such an experience, it is obvious and self-evident. This is the kind of argument that drives dispassionate scholars of religion and philosophers mad, given that there is no objective measure by which to judge the claim. Yet, it is a claim that spiritual practitioners easily accept. Denying the fundamental reality of such experiences, for those who have had such an experience, is tantamount to denying reality itself.

Perceiving Reality As It Is

THIS SELF-EVIDENT TRUTH of the mushroom experience bears much in common with mystical experience. In essence, the mystical experience is understood to be direct perception of the fundamental nature of reality as an undivided whole. In this state, there is no subject, no object. There is only the basic suchness of being. This state is often described as being beyond any mental or experiential constructs of space and time. Mystical awareness is not bound by any limits of ordinary experience. Furthermore, the mystical experience is associated with profound affective states of joy, universal compassion, a sense of completeness, fulfillment, and total acceptance and love. And, as virtually all mystics agree, the experience itself is fundamentally ineffable. Any attempt to describe this state is only a partial reconstruction after the fact. There are no words, concepts, or conventional means to accurately describe mystical awareness. For the mystical experience to truly be understood, one must experience it for one's self.

The mystical experience is associated with profound affective states of joy, universal compassion, a sense of completeness, fulfillment, and total acceptance and love.

Religion and Entheogens

DIFFERENT RELIGIOUS TRADITIONS have different methods and techniques for arriving at a mystical state of consciousness. These include sustained prayer, meditation, fasting, self-deprivation, isolation, physical hardship, and other such techniques. While most organized religions frown upon the use of entheogens, there is good reason to believe that the origins of religion in general were connected to ancient use of entheogens. In the mainstream religions, use of entheogens is often seen as a false attempt to arrive at a mystical experience through expedient methods. Mystical consciousness is generally seen as the product of years—even a lifetime—of sustained practice and dedication.

That entheogens appear to open up radical states of mystical awareness in those who consume them seems to indicate that anyone can have a mystical experience and that religious proscriptions of morality, ethical behavior, adherence to dogma or profession of faith, have little, if anything, to do with receiving mystical grace. Given that many religions exhort their followers to be, think, and act in certain ways to receive the grace of a higher power, the universalizing factor of entheogens presents a major threat to religious hegemony of spiritual experience and practice. In other words, entheogenic experience makes the arbitrariness of much of religious dogma obvious and clearly apparent.

Mushrooms and Mysticism

IDEAS OF HAVING A "CLEAN HEART" and identifying one's heart with the "heart of the universe" and experiencing a "free flow of Spirit" can be described as parts of the mystical experience. Here, spiritual practitioners seek to transcend limiting concepts of self and identity, to open awareness of a fundamental nature of being that exists behind appearances of manifesting reality, and to invite that fundamental reality of Spirit to shape the course of their life and experience in the manifest world. In other words, this is a description of methods of practice that are designed to bring a practitioner's awareness back to the source of being and letting that source of being transform the practitioner's sense of self, being, and world.

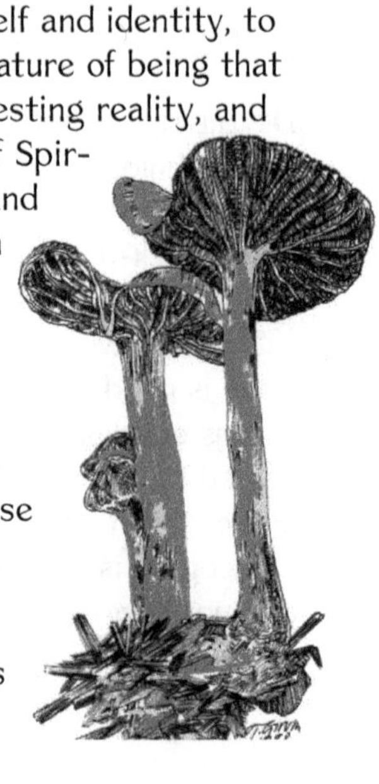

However, it is important to emphasize that the "clean heart" is not a dogma of ethics or morality.

It is about honest recognition of one's behavior and the consequences of choices and actions. It is about a level of awareness of how the spiritual seeker affects others and the whole of reality. This is not promoting and ethical system of "do's" and "don't's." It is promoting a sense of action based on recognition of the fundamental interconnectedness of all things. All actions, decisions, and behaviors have consequences and affect the world and others and are reflected back to one in the mushroom trance when looking in the spiritual mirror. In the mushroom revelation, when we come to understand how all manifest things are interconnected and ultimately generated from the same universal source of being, then if we are to act with conscious awareness, we naturally act in such a way that takes the effects of our actions into consideration. Ethical behavior is predicated on the perception of unity and interconnection, not on moralistic superstructures of right and wrong, good and bad.

Full mystical awareness is difficult, if not impossible, to maintain for long periods of time, especially when we must function in the world.

The process of cleaning out our hearts is a process of overcoming self-limiting constructs that spiritual practitioners have created or accepted for their self that impede their ability to connect to that universal source of being, or divine consciousness. The wounded heart, one filled with pain, suffering, and judgment, traps the spiritual seeker into cycles of judgment, blame, and criticism of self and others. The wounded heart sees the world in oppositional, not unifying, terms. When the heart is cleaned out,

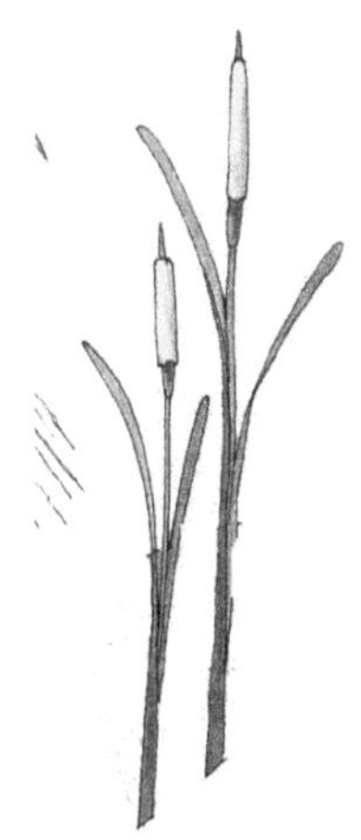

mystical communion with the heart of the universe, the fundamental ground of being, becomes possible. We can describe this as an experience of grace.

Once such an experience and level of realization is achieved, the spiritual seeker generally undergoes a profound shift in identity. The constructs of ego are seen for what they are—constructs, illusions, masks, and conventional realities. The true nature of being transcends all these limiting factors. The spiritual seeker learns that our normal sources of identity are all only partially true and authentic, at best, and that our core of being is something much deeper and fundamentally universal.

Full mystical awareness is difficult, if not impossible, to maintain for long periods of time, especially when we must function in the world. There has to be some distance from the source, for the full mystical experience is contentless—beyond subject and object.

What is profound about the mushroom experience is that it reminds the spiritual seeker that this fundamental ground of being is universally present, and that our connection to it is manifested through creative acts in the world of subject and object. The ground of being is profoundly creative, and our participation with that source is creative as well. We express our sense of creativity through action, art, and expressive endeavors. These are the practices that allow us to manifest that sense of universal being in ordinary states of consciousness. In other words, the mushroom experience can bring us to a mystical state of consciousness, as well as help guide the seeker along the path of realizing a certain degree of that consciousness in everyday life through spiritual practice and expressive action.

Shamanism

Shamanism is directed towards definite ends, such as healing, divination, influencing local spirits, and not salvation.

"MYSTICISM" AND MYSTICAL EXPERIENCE are most commonly associated with organized religions by scholars of religion, while "shamanism" is most commonly associated with indigenous traditions across the globe. This is a good distinction for the most part. There do seem to be differences in systems of practice between highly organized religions and the religions of indigenous communities and their overwhelming focus on local, place-based religions. On the other hand, this is a bad distinction in that shamanism is most likely the root of all religion and therefore most likely the root of mystical experience as well. In this sense, mystical experience is a refined state of shamanic consciousness that has been given special importance by the organized religions, whereas it might not be so highly valued by the shamans themselves. This is primarily due to the fact that shamanism is ultimately pragmatic and purpose driven, being based in local contexts where the shaman's services are needed by the community, whereas mystical consciousness is more about personal revelation or salvation at the direction of a sanctified church or institution. Ultimately, shamanism is directed towards definite ends, such as healing, divination, influencing local spirits, and not salvation. Some organized religions, such as Tantric Buddhism and Taoism, still have a great deal of shamanic influence in them and make use of shamanic methodologies, while others, such as Christianity, have very little.

There are many shamanic traditions around the world and they exhibit a wide degree of variability and innovation. Indigenous shamanism is always closely associated with local religious traditions, meaning that the shaman works in a context of local rituals, sacred stories, and belief systems. However, at the core, there are certain techniques and practices that appear to be nearly universal, which is why the term of "shaman" has some legitimacy as a universal scholarly and cultural term to refer to certain categories of spiritual practitioners.

The shaman makes use of altered states of consciousness to affect consensual reality, retrieve information, seek spiritual knowledge, perform healing sessions, and affect local spirits for the purpose of influencing the weather, plant growth, ecological balance, or whatever the need might be.

Anthropologists studying shamanism in its traditional contexts coined the term "neo-shamanism," for the techniques and methods of traditional shamanism that have been incorporated into the spiritual practices of non-indigenous people in industrialized societies. Uses of drumming, fasting, forms of purification, and, of course, ingestion of entheogenic substances all fall into this category when used outside of the context of an indigenous culture.

Shamanic Consciousness

THE SHAMAN MAKES USE of altered states of consciousness to affect consensual reality, retrieve information, seek spiritual knowledge, perform healing sessions, and affect local spirits for the purpose of influencing the weather, plant growth, ecological balance, or whatever the need might be. To achieve these ends, shamans use trance states of consciousness to contact the spirit world, which is the realm in which they are the most effective as spiritual agents. Shamans travel into the spirit world through the power of their minds to bring benefits and knowledge into this realm.

It is likely that use of entheogens was the first form of shamanism. Many cultures retained this form of shamanism while others moved to less reliable and less effective techniques to achieve spiritual states of consciousness, such as through drumming, fasting, and sensory deprivation.

Shamans see all of existence as a kind of great communal dream and within it there is no such thing as lifeless matter or inanimate objects, devoid of spirit and life.

Regardless of the method, shamans explore the realms of altered states of consciousness to gain insight and wisdom. Shamans do not explore altered states of consciousness for the sake of experience, but rather for what they can do with it. When their consciousness is altered, they are able to gain information through experiences that might be labeled astral projection, telepathy, clairvoyance, clairaudience, divination, oracular prophecy, possession, and channeling. Shamans use this information to make changes in consensual reality by healing a patient, finding lost objects, or bringing ecological balance to local environments and bringing the local human community into balance with vegetable, animal, atmospheric, and mineral spheres of life. In this sense, shamans promote mystical awareness if they see a benefit to it. Otherwise, such a refined state of consciousness might not be promoted by a shaman as the practical is the ultimate concern.

Spirit in All Things

A basic shamanic axiom is that all things participate in Spirit and consciousness. All of existence is seen as a kind of great communal dream and within it there is no such thing as lifeless matter or inanimate objects, devoid of spirit and life. All things are alive, in some sense, and participate in Spirit and the great continual unfolding of the universe. Because of this reality, all things carry knowledge, information, and various degrees of power.

Shamans seek out different symbols, objects, and spiritual agents to serve as allies and tools of power to navigate the spirit world and manipulate and transform the forces and elements found there.

Multiple Realities

ANOTHER BASIC AXIOM OF SHAMANISM is that there are multiple dimensions to reality, most of which are not normally apparent. We gain access to these realms through symbols, ritual, chant, music, and entheogens. Within these realms there are different spirit powers, different forms of consciousness, and different forms of spiritual agency. These levels of reality might be described as parallel universes, or different "worlds," such as lower, middle, and upper realm. In ecstatic flight, when deep in an entheogen trance, the shaman travels through these alternate worlds to make contact with the spirit forces within them to learn from them, gain knowledge, or receive gifts of empowerment. This learning is translated into the realm of consensual reality through song, story, symbol, and ritual action.

Shamanic Sound

AN IMPORTANT ASPECT OF SHAMANISM is manipulation of sound. In many respects, the alternate dimensions of consciousness and reality are affected by sound. When shamans sing, they are not singing their own songs, for example. They are evoking spirit forces that resonate between dimensions, giving a vibratory shape and form through which the spirit force can express itself in consensual reality. Using sound, shamans can manifest spiritual forces, transport others into altered states or realms, call spirits to a healing session, and communicate with the intelligences embodied within the environment or greater nature. When the shaman speaks

Shamans use sound to drive the spiritual experience.

and sings, it is with the authority of Spirit, not the projection of ego. Sound, just like all things for the shaman, is a spiritual tool that is put to work in the service of Spirit.

Sound is crucial for the shaman's experience as it serves to drive spiritual experience. Drumming, rattling, chanting, all resonate deeply in the mushroom trance, for example, and through the careful manipulation of sound, the shaman travels between realms. It is common, for example, for indigenous shamans to refer to their drums as horses. The sound of the drum is like a galloping horse, carrying them through the altered realms of the spirit world. It sustains them in transformed shape as they fly through the heavens or swim beneath the spiritual sea. Sound is a vehicle for spirit travel, and through travel, the shaman learns and gains insight.

Mushrooms and Shamanism

USING MUSHROOMS AS AN ALLY, for example, is decidedly shamanic. So too is the use of drumming, rattling, or sonic stimulation of mushroom states of consciousness. The shaman is the purposeful explorer of altered states of consciousness, and always makes use of allies and ritual tools to do so. Mushroom eaters who explore and enter the realms opened up by mushroom with similar intent and methodology are engaging in shamanic practices, regardless of whether the mushroom eater is properly a "shaman" or not.

Shamanic Mysticism

THE END CONCLUSION must therefore be that mushrooms make both shamanic and mystical states of consciousness open to mushroom eaters. If we were to give them a label, the techniques and practices described in this book might best be called "shamanic mysticism," as it partakes of elements of both. Most spiritual practitioners will probably gravitate more towards one form of spiritual experience or the other. Mystical experience is more amenable to solitary practitioners, or those seeking personal transformation and enlightenment.

Shamanic practice is more suitable for those who are interested in exploring the multifaceted realms of mushroom consciousness and for those who are drawn to work with others in a healing or otherwise "shamanic" capacity. Both mystical experience and shamanic experience are empowered by having a clean heart, clear intentions, and focused awareness. Any spiritual practitioner, of any inclination, is wise to look in the spiritual mirror and take a good hard look at what is found there, and let those lessons shape the course of one's spiritual path. May it be done with openness, honesty, compassion, and full awareness of the great mystery that surrounds and envelops us all.

Chapter 15, Main Points:

* Shamanism and mysticism are two related categories of spiritual experience.

* Mysticism is most closely associated with organized religions and shamanism with indigenous traditions.

* Mystical states of consciousness are refined states of shamanic awareness.

* Mystical states are ineffable and universal.

* Mystical states and experiences are communicated through specific traditions and cultures.

* Mystical awareness is an experience of transcending subject and object and directly perceiving the nature of reality.

* Shamans are primarily practical: they use altered states of consciousness to affect change in consensus reality.

* Shamans are masters of consciousness. They explore the spirit world and different aspects of consciousness in their work.

* Shamans see everything as imbued with life, spirit, and consciousness. There is no such thing as dead matter in the shamanic worldview.

* Shamans use ritual, sound, and spiritual tools to affect change and bring about positive results.

Recommended Reading:

Mushrooms

Teonanacatl: Sacred Mushrooms of Vision, Ralph Metzner, Park Street, 2005

Magic Mushrooms in Religion and Alchemy, Clak Heinrich, Park Street, 2002

The Wondrous Mushroom, R. Gordon Wasson, McGraw Hill, 1980

Psilocybin Mushrooms of the World, Paul Stamets, Ten Speed, 1996

Mushrooms and Mankind, James Arthur, The Book Tree, 2003

Entheogens

Plants of the Gods: Their Sacred, Healing, and Hallucinogenic Powers, Richard Evans Schultes, Healing Arts Press, 2001

Psychedelic Shamanism, Jim Dekorne, Breakout Production, 1994

Sacred Vine of Spirits: Ayahuasca, Ralph Metzner, Park Street, 2005

Ayahuasca: Human Consciousness and the Spirit of Nature, Ralph Metzner, Thunder's Mouth, 1999

The Cosmic Serpent, Jeremy Narby, Tarcher, 1999

Tales of a Shaman's Apprentice, Mark J. Plotkin, Penguin, 1994

True Hallucinations, Terence McKenna, HarperSan-Francisco, 1994

The Food of the Gods, Terence McKenna, Bantam, 1993

Flesh of the Gods, Peter Furst, Waveland, 1990

The World As You Dream It, John Perkins, Destiny Books, 1994

DMT: the Spirit Molecule, Rick Strassman, Park Street, 2000

Shamanism

Shamanic Voices, Joan Halifax, Penguin, 1991

Shamanism and Tantra in the Himalayas, Surendra Bahadur Shahi et al, Inner Traditions, 2002

The Fruitful Darkness, Joan Halifax, Grove, 2004

Hallucinogens and Shamanism, Michael Harner, Oxford University Press, 1973

The Shaman in the Woman's Body, Barbara Tedlock, Bantam, 2005

Shamanism: Archaic Techniques of Ecstasy, Mircae Eliade, Princeton University Press, 2004

The Way of the Shaman, Michael Harner, HarperSan-Francisco, 1990

Peyote Hunt, Barbara Myerhoff, Cornell University Press, 1976

Cracking Open the Head, Daniel Pinchbeck, Broadway, 2003

Urban Shaman, Serge Kahili King, Fireside, 1990

Shamans, Healers, and Medicine Men, Holger Kalweit, Shambhala, 2000

Physics, Science, and Philosophy

Parallel Universes, Fred Alan Wolf, Simon and Shuster, 1990

Phenomenology of Perception, Maurice Merleau-Ponty, Routledge, 2002

Metapatterns, Tyler Volk, Columbia U. Press, 1995

Mutual Causality in Buddhism and General Systems Theory, Joanna Macy, State University NY Press, 1991

The Quantum Self, Danah Zohar, Harper Perennial, 1991

The Elegant Universe, Brian Green, Vintage, 2000

Hyperspace Michio Kaku, Anchorday, 1994

The Self-Aware Universe, Amit Goswami, Tarcher, 1995

Choosing Reality, B. Alan Wallace, Snow Lion, 2003

Mysticism

Mysticism and Philosophical Analysis, Steven Katz, Oxford University. Press, 1978

The Mystical Mind, Eugene G. D'Aquili et al, Augsburg Fortress, 1999

Exploring Mysticism, Fritz Staal, University of California Press, 1975

About the Author

Martin W. Ball, Ph.D., holds a doctorate in Religious Studies with an emphasis on Native American religions and spiritual traditions, comparative mysticism, and shamanism. He studied ritual and traditional healing with the Mescalero Apache medicine people in New Mexico. Martin is an avid musician/composer and plays didjeridu, percussion, and Native American flute. He lives in the Santa Ynez Valley in southern California with his wife and daughter.

Tales of Aurduin
Orobal's Vision

$14.95, 270 pages
An inspiring shamanic fable, with deep spiritual and philosophical themes, in which Orobai, the sole remaining practitioner of the Illan's mystical art of creation, seeks a vision to guide him in piecing together the intricate puzzle of his fate, the identity of a mysterious young girl, and healing the devastating ecological sickness overtaking Aurduin in the aftermath of a prophesized apocalypse.

Infinite Horizons

$12.98, Audio CD
Shamanic rhythms and vast, meditative soundscapes with didjeridu, throat and overtone singing compsed and performed by Martin Bell.
1. Stars in My Hands 2. Didjscape 3. Ecstatic Moment 4. Raven 5. Festival of Waters 6. Four Winds 7. In the Lair of the Mystic Toad 8. Manjushri 9. Shapeshifting 10. Just Wind.

These and Dr. Ball's other creations are available from his website: www.martinball.net.

When Spirit flows through us, we cannot help but to be a creative force.

www.ingramcontent.com/pod-product-compliance
Lightning Source LLC
Jackson TN
JSHW011654231224
75956JS00003B/23

* 9 7 8 1 5 7 9 5 1 0 3 6 7 *